# POEMS OF GÓNGORA

# POEMS OF
# GÓNGORA

SELECTED, INTRODUCED AND
ANNOTATED BY

R.O.JONES
*Cervantes Professor of Spanish*
*King's College, University of London*

CAMBRIDGE
AT THE UNIVERSITY PRESS
1966

PUBLISHED BY
THE SYNDICS OF THE CAMBRIDGE UNIVERSITY PRESS
Bentley House, 200 Euston Road, London, N.W. 1
American Branch: 32 East 57th Street, New York, N.Y. 10022
West African Office: P.M.B. 5181, Ibadan, Nigeria



*The portrait on the cover is reproduced by permission of the Boston Museum of Fine Arts, Boston, Mass.*

*Printed in Great Britain at the University Printing House, Cambridge (Brooke Crutchley, University Printer)*

LIBRARY OF CONGRESS CATALOGUE
CARD NUMBER: 66–10733

# CONTENTS

# PREFACE

Any study of Góngora must begin with an acknowledgement to Dámaso Alonso's many and fundamental writings on the poet. I gladly acknowledge my debt. I am also grateful for permission to use his text of the *Soledad Primera* and of the *Fábula de Polifemo y Galatea*. I wish to record a special debt, however, to Professor Edward M. Wilson, from whom I learned, first as pupil and then as colleague, to appreciate Góngora.

This selection of poems will look very familiar: space was limited, and deliberately to choose the less admired poems would have been eccentric. In the introduction only an outline of a general study could be attempted: exhaustive stylistic analysis of the poems discussed was impossible in a few pages. The notes are intended to help with difficult constructions, unfamiliar connotations, and strange allusions. Access to a dictionary and some general knowledge on the part of the student had to be taken for granted.

R. O. J.

*London*

# INTRODUCTION

## 1 BIOGRAPHY

Don Luis de Góngora y Argote was born in Córdoba on 11 July 1561.[1] Both his parents, Don Francisco de Argote and Doña Leonor de Góngora, were of ancient and noble family. Don Francisco was himself a highly cultivated man of letters and one of the foremost citizens of the Córdoba of his day. To advantages of birth were joined those of education. Góngora was sent to the Jesuit school in Córdoba and then, in 1576, to the University of Salamanca. To pay for his studies his maternal uncle, Don Francisco de Góngora, a prebendary of Córdoba Cathedral, made some of his benefices over to the young Góngora, who took minor orders for the purpose.

At Salamanca, Góngora appears to have devoted himself less to his studies than to poetry, cards and other unacademic pursuits; at all events, having run through a very considerable sum of money, he left the university in 1580 without a degree. (He may have taken a degree in later years elsewhere.) His uncle Don Francisco renounced his prebend in favour of Góngora who, in order to enter into his full rights, took deacon's orders in 1586.

Góngora was probably not a model member of his Chapter. He had critics: in 1588 he was charged before the bishop with frequent absences, with talking during divine service, with idle gossiping and attending bullfights. The list ended: 'vive, en fin, como muy mozo y anda de día y de noche en cosas ligeras; trata representantes de comedias, y escribe coplas profanas.' Góngora's tongue-in-cheek defence was that his absences were always with just cause; that 'he estado siempre en las Horas con tanto silencio como el que más; pero aun cuando quiera no estar con el que se me manda, tengo a mis lados un sordo y uno que jamás cesa de cantar, y así callo por no tener quien me responda'. He denied the charge of idle gossiping and affirmed that he went to bull-

[1] I am indebted throughout to the biography of Góngora by Artigas and to the works of Dámaso Alonso (see book list). References to the works of Góngora not in the anthology are (by number) to his *Obras completas*, edited by Juan and Isabel Millé y Giménez (Madrid, n.d. My references to 1943 edition).

fights in the company of 'personas de más años y más órdenes que yo'; he added that 'ni mi vida es tan escandalosa ni yo tan viejo que se me pueda acusar de vivir como mozo'; and that people of the theatre resorted to his house because of his love for music. Finally, concerning his poetry, he said: 'Que aunque es verdad que en el hacer coplas he tenido alguna libertad, no ha sido tanta como la que se me carga; porque las más Letrillas que me achacan no son mías...; y que si mi poesía no ha sido tan espiritual como debiera, que mi poca Theología me disculpa, pues es tan poca, que he tenido por mejor ser condenado por liviano que por hereje.' In his findings the Bishop commanded him to keep away from bullfights and fined him four ducats for charitable works.

Góngora almost certainly had some love affairs as a student and in later years. Some at least of his many amorous poems seem to be addressed to real women and to reflect real feeling. This side of Góngora is perhaps to be glimpsed in the romance *Hanme dicho hermanas* (1587)—though not too much weight is to be given to this burlesque piece:

> Es su Reverencia
> un gran coronista,
> porque en Salamanca
> oyó teología,
> sin perder mañana
> su lección de prima,
> y al anochecer
> lección de sobrina. (Millé, 24)

(*Prima*, 'Prime', and also the term for the top string of a guitar—an allusion to Góngora's well-known love of music. He both composed and played.) The evidence of Góngora's life and works seems to show that his Orders did not sit too heavily on his conscience.

Nevertheless, Góngora enjoyed the confidence of his Chapter on whose behalf he made many and frequent business journeys up and down Spain, journeys that one can easily suppose to have been a welcome change from the narrowness of provincial life.

Góngora's life passed in this way until 1617, when he moved to Madrid and was granted a royal chaplaincy (for which at last he had to be ordained priest). This he hoped was only the beginning of his rise. His hopes were not to be realised. His life in Madrid was one of bitter disappointments and financial distress, no doubt aggravated by his passion for cards, which never left him (and which gave Quevedo an opening for some of his cruellest satires). He lacked the gift of attaching himself to the right party. He pinned his early hopes on the Duque de Lerma and Rodrigo Calderón, and was soon to be disabused by their disgrace and the subsequent execution of the second. The letters Góngora sent during his Madrid years to Cristóbal de Heredia, who administered his affairs in Córdoba, give a poignant picture of disappointment and hardship, made the more bitter by the ingratitude of members of his family to whom he had shown great generosity.

In 1625 he had a stroke. He survived, but with his memory impaired. In 1626 he returned to Córdoba and died there on 23 May 1627.

The first poem of Góngora's that appeared in print, the first indeed that can be dated, appeared in the preliminaries of a translation of the *Lusiads* published by Luis Gómez de Tapia in 1580. Other poems were to appear (often anonymously) in collections like the *Romancero general* (1600) and Pedro Espinosa's *Flores de ilustres poetas* (1605), but for the most part Góngora's poems circulated in manuscript. He was already well known as a poet when in 1613 he sent to friends in Madrid a draft of the first *Soledad* (the second probably not yet written) and of the *Fábula de Polifemo y Galatea* (perhaps written in 1612). Through the imprudence of one of the recipients the poems were made public and became at once the centre of excited controversy. Góngora had already provoked the enmity of Lope de Vega and Quevedo; now new enemies arose. Góngora was attacked by Juan de Jáuregui in his *Antídoto contra la pestilente poesía de las 'Soledades'* (probably written in 1614), which was attacked in its turn by Francisco Fernández de Córdoba, Abad de Rute, in his *Examen del Antídoto*.[1] These were the opening shots of a long war, in which Góngora was enthusiastically defended by seventeenth-century commentators on his works like Pedro Díaz de Rivas,

[1] For the text of the *Examen*, see Artigas, pp. 400–67; for the *Antídoto* see Eunice Joiner Gates, *Documentos gongorinos* (Mexico, 1960).

José Pellicer de Salas y Tovar, García de Salcedo Coronel and others.[1]

In his last years Góngora began gathering his poems for publication. He died without realising his plan. Shortly after his death, Juan López de Vicuña brought out an edition under the title *Obras en verso del Homero español* (Madrid, 1627). Its sale was prohibited by the Inquisition on the grounds that much of the poetry was excessively scurrilous and irreligious. Behind this action lay the rancour of a priest whose path Góngora had crossed years before.[2] Another edition of Góngora's works was brought out some years later by Gonzalo Hoces y Córdoba under the title *Todas las obras de don Luis de Góngora* (Madrid, 1633).

Though he was much attacked, Góngora lived to see his style imitated even by his enemies. *Gongorismo* left its mark on a great part of the literature of the seventeenth century. Góngora's elaborate poems fell into disfavour, however, in the eighteenth and nineteenth centuries and it was not until the twentieth that his poetry came again to be esteemed. This was due to the work of numerous scholars, among whom Dámaso Alonso stands out. His edition of the *Soledades* in 1927 was at once an important work of scholarship and a poetic manifesto. The *Soledades*, the quintessence of Góngora and his most ambitious work, were acclaimed as *puramente poéticas*, the embodiment of *pura belleza*, and were defended in terms that announced the aesthetic ideals of a generation of poets of whom Dámaso Alonso was one.

## 2 GÓNGORA'S POETRY

Góngora's verse is of many kinds: amorous, heroic, pastoral, satirical (and often very scurrilous), religious (though the religious poems, chiefly on the Nativity, are relatively few). He wrote, too, in a number of verse-forms, including sonnets, *romances* (lines of eight—sometimes six—syllables with alternate assonance), *letrillas*

[1] Artigas, pp. 227–45. The principal commentaries are: José García de Salcedo Coronel, *Soledades...comentadas* (1636), *El Polifemo...comentado* (1636), *Obras... comentadas* (1645); José Pellicer, *Lecciones solemnes a las obras de Don Luis de Góngora* (1630); Pedro Díaz de Rivas, *Discursos apologéticos*, in E. Joiner Gates, *op. cit.*

[2] Artigas, pp. 205–12; and the introduction by Dámaso Alonso to the facsimile of Vicuña's edition (Madrid, 1963). The most scurrilous poems in Vicuña's edition were not in fact by Góngora.

(composed in traditional metres—eight- or six-syllable lines—of varying stanza form with a repeated *estribillo* or refrain), *silvas* (a free combination of seven- and eleven-syllable lines with no set rhyme-scheme), etc.

Góngora's style, too, is varied. Some, though by no means all, of his *romances* and *letrillas* are simple and direct in style. Others of his works are written in a *culto* style of enormous artificiality and difficulty abounding in Latinisms of vocabulary and construction, classical allusions, and tropes of all kinds. The *culto* poems are the ones which caused controversy; the more simple poems seem to have been universally admired. Too hard and fast a distinction should not be made between the two styles: few of the 'simple' poems are completely straightforward; certainly, a chronological division into 'early' and 'late' would be quite wrong since even the earliest poems exhibit strikingly *culto* features. Nevertheless, it is true that Góngora's *culto* verse became progressively more difficult as time went on until it reached its climax in the great poems of 1612–13.

It would be wrong to play down the contribution of Góngora's own personality to the development of this style; all the same, the creation of the style was not simply an idiosyncrasy of Góngora's. Most of the elements of Góngora's *culto* style have precedents in earlier Spanish poets such as Herrera and others of his generation who attempted to create a distinctively poetic diction purged of the colloquial and everyday. What Góngora did was to make a more intensive and systematic use of those elements; and make of them better poetry. Italian poetry of the sixteenth century, in which Góngora was steeped, shows a movement in a parallel direction.

Góngora's intention was, in part, to confer on Spanish poetry the perfection and prestige that Latin possessed for sixteenth- and seventeenth-century Europe. In a letter he wrote in 1613 or 1614 in defence of the *Soledades* he said: 'De honroso, en dos maneras considero me ha sido honrosa esta poesía; si entendida para los doctos, causarme ha autoridad, siendo lance forzoso venerar que nuestra lengua a costa de mi trabajo haya llegado a la perfección y alteza de la latina...' (Millé, letter no. 2). At the same time, the obscurity of the poetry was a deliberate attempt to make it incomprehensible to the many. He wrote in the same letter:

'Demás que honra me ha causado hacerme escuro a los ignorantes, que esa es la distinción de los hombres doctos, hablar de manera que a ellos les parezca griego....' Here again Góngora's views were no novelty. In his treatise *El libro de la erudición poética* (1611) Luis Carrillo de Sotomayor had written in a similar vein: 'Eternidad y valor prometen las Musas, joyas por cierto bien preciosas.... Con el tiempo andan olvidadas, y lo anduvieron tanto que se atrevieron a profanar de sus sagrados templos las más preciosas joyas. Presume el vulgo de entendellas, el mismo pretende juzgallas....Engañóse por cierto quien entiende los trabajos de la Poesía haber nacido para el vulgo.' In this, then, Góngora was following the current of his times.

The importance of the doctrine of imitation in Renaissance Europe has to be borne firmly in mind by the modern reader if Góngora is not to be accused of lacking a kind of originality that he did not wish to possess. The Renaissance poet, despairing of improving on the great classical poets whom he revered, took them as his model, to be imitated when possible, to be borrowed from when necessary. This did not mean slavish imitation of the classical models, however: Renaissance practice was more like variations on a ground. To the canon of models to be imitated modern poets were added as they acquired the status of classics. Petrarch is one of the most noteworthy examples. Garcilaso acquired this status within the sixteenth century. Góngora, then, his mind richly stocked with the literatures of Classical Antiquity and the Renaissance, viewed life 'through the spectacles of books' (as Johnson said of Milton)—or at least he wrote as if he did. Even when describing the most everyday object or event his mind was full of precedents, models and allusions. When mentioning a goatherd's wooden spoon in the *Soledades* (I, 152) he cannot refrain from alluding to Virgil. If he had been called on to justify this he might have done so in the words of one whom he must have heard lecture at Salamanca—Francisco Sánchez, *El Brocense*, who in his edition of the works of Garcilaso had written: '...digo, y afirmo, que no tengo por buen poeta al que no imita los excelentes antiguos. Y si me preguntan por qué entre tantos millares de poetas como nuestra España tiene, tan pocos se pueden contar dignos de este nombre, digo que no hay otra razón sino porque les faltan las ciencias, lenguas y doctrina para saber imitar. Ningún poeta latino hay que en su género no haya imitado a otros....Lo mismo se puede decir de nuestro Poeta, que aplica y traslada los versos y sentencias de otros poetas tan a su propósito, y con tanta destreza, que ya no se llaman ajenos sino suyos; y más gloria merece por esto, que si no de su cabeza lo compusiera, como lo afirma Horacio en su Arte Poética.'

This, which looks like unbearable pedantry to a modern reader, was accepted doctrine.

It is clear to any reader of Góngora's major poems that he imitated not only individual Latin poets but the Latin language itself. The poetry is heavy with Latinisms, many of them neologisms (though many had been used in the fifteenth century by Juan de Mena): *canoro*, *crepúsculo*, *estrépito*, *nocturno*, *ebúrneo*, *purpúreo*, *vulto* ('face'), etc. Many of these neologisms have since passed into normal usage. Góngora made constant use, too, of hyperbaton, a rhetorical figure in which the normal word order is inverted and related parts of speech are separated (an article from its noun, a noun from its adjective, etc.). Quevedo satirised these characteristics of Góngora's style in a sonnet:

> Quien quisiere ser culto en solo un día,
> la jeri- (aprenderá) gonza siguiente:
> *fulgores*, *arrogar*, *joven*, *presiente*,
> *candor*, *construye*, *métrica armonía*;
> *poco*, *mucho*, *si no*, *purpuracía*,
> *neutralidad*, *conculca*, *erige*, *mente*,
> *pulsa*, *ostenta*, *librar*, *adolescente*,
> *señas traslada*, *pira*, *frustra*, *harpía*,
> *cede*, *impide*, *cisuras*, *petulante*,
> *palestra*, *liba*, *meta*, *argento*, *alterna*,
> *si bien*, *disuelve*, *émulo*, *canoro*.
> Use mucho de *líquido* y de *errante*,
> su poco de *nocturno* y de *caverna*,
> anden listos *livor*, *adunco* y *poro*.

Another figure much used by Góngora is the Greek accusative:

> — lasciva el movimiento,
> mas los ojos honesta — (*Soledad* I, 256–7)

('her movements lascivious but her eyes chaste').

Góngora makes much use of constructions with *si no* or *si*.

*Si no* (to take the most typical form of the construction) usually implies antithesis, as when Góngora describes a labyrinth of nets:

laberinto nudoso de marino
Dédalo, si de leño no, de lino. (*Soledad* II, 77–8)

On other occasions, however, the construction may express not difference but equivalence, as in:

sirena dulce si no esfinge bella. (Millé, 338)

The lady described is *both* siren *and* Sphinx. As a result of this dual use, this construction—one of Góngora's stylistic idiosyncrasies—can be a source of difficulty to a reader not yet familiar with Góngora's poetry.

Innumerable classical allusions form the basis of Góngora's constant use of periphrasis: the description of things not directly but allusively, in terms of their attributes and associations. From all these elements he could make overwhelmingly expressive poetry, as when he describes with great erotic effect how Galatea delicately eludes the caresses of Acis, who burns for her as passionately as Tantalus had thirsted for the water that eternally receded from his mouth, and who tries to touch her breasts—*pomos de nieve*—as Tantalus had tried to pluck the fruit that slipped for ever from his grasp.

Entre las ondas y la fruta, imita
Acis el siempre ayuno en penas graves:
que, en tanta gloria, infierno son no breve
fugitivo cristal, pomos de nieve. (*Polifemo*, 325–8)

*Gongorismo* has often been loosely equated with empty adornment; what these lines show is economy and compression.

Hyperbaton, too, can become powerfully expressive in Góngora's hands. To take one instance: when at the beginning of the first *Soledad* the shipwrecked youth scales the cliff, Góngora holds back the verb *escala* for line after line until, when at last it comes, at the very end of the passage, we feel the full force of the youth's mingled triumph and relief as victoriously he reaches the top:

No bien pues de su luz los horizontes
— que hacían desigual, confusamente
montes de agua y piélagos de montes —
desdorados los siente,

cuando — entregado el mísero extranjero
en lo que ya del mar redimió fiero —
entre espinas crepúsculos pisando,
riscos que aun igualara mal, volando,
veloz, intrépida ala,
— menos cansado que confuso — escala.

(*Soledad* I, 42–51)

Another characteristic of Góngora's poetry is his intensified use of the commonplace similes of Renaissance poetry so as to create out of them a poetic language of his own. By accepting as his normal means of expression what were the poetic adjectives and images of his predecessors, it is (in Dámaso Alonso's image) as if he started climbing not from sea-level but from a plateau. When he speaks of the white limbs of a country girl he calls them *nieve* or *cristal*. Galatea's arms as she clings to Acis are *cristalinos pámpanos*. In this way poetic commonplaces are compressed into a new style of poetry by Góngora's turning simile into metaphor, so that white skin is not merely *like* snow but *is* snow. In this system of his, anything white—fleece, skin, flax, linen, snow—could be described by the same metaphors, and the metaphors were interchangeable, so that any one of the terms could stand for any other. Other colours have their metaphors too; blood could be *rubí*, red lips *claveles*, ripe corn *oro*, etc. The richness and compression that Góngora was able to achieve may be judged in lines like these:

De cuantos siegan oro, esquilan nieve,
o en pipas guardan la exprimida grana,
bien sea religión, bien amor sea,
deidad, aunque sin templo, es Galatea.

(*Polifemo*, 149–52)

It may be objected that by doing this Góngora has taken away individuality from whatever he describes: the particular is merged in the generic, the universal. This is true; but it may very well have formed part of Góngora's purpose. He seems in his 'generic' imagery to be attempting to capture the essence that lies behind the particular. This is perhaps alluded to when he hints in the letter referred to earlier (Millé, letter 2) that the *Soledades* were concerned in some way with *la primera verdad* and that in his poetry are to be found 'debajo de las sombras de la obscuridad asimilaciones a su concepto (i.e. approximations or resemblances *al concepto* [*de*] *la primera verdad*). Behind all this there is more than an echo of the Platonic Ideas. At the heart of the sixteenth-century discussions that went on around Aristotle's rediscovered *Poetics* there is often to be found a Platonic core. In his *Discorsi* Tasso drew a parallel between the poet and the mystical theologian. Both 'make images' of truth or reality. 'Wherefore to lead to the contemplation of divine things and to awaken in this way with images, as do the mystical theologian and the poet, is a much more noble task than to instruct with demonstrations, as is the office of the scholastic theologian.' The poet's images or representations are of 'subsisting things'. Tasso goes on: 'But what things shall we say to be subsisting things—the intelligible or the visible? Intelligible things, surely, and once again on the authority of Plato, who placed visible things in the category of non-being, and only intelligible things did he place in the category of being' (*nel genere de gli enti*).[1] Aristotle, the acknowledged authority in the sixteenth century since Robortelli's commentary on the *Poetics* (1548), was taken to affirm that whereas history was concerned with particulars (things as they occurred), poetry was concerned with universals (the probable, the typical as opposed to the accidental). By giving this version of Aristotle's doctrine a Platonic interpretation, Tasso is able to suggest that the poet is concerned with a reality—Plato's realm of eternal Ideas—behind appearances. Góngora knew Tasso's poetry well; it is possible and even probable that he knew these *Discorsi*, which became very well known after their publication in 1594. Certainly, Góngora's cloudy pronouncements in the letter quoted above point back to some such source.

These, then, are the chief characteristics of Góngora's *culto* style (to which the word *culterano*—modelled on *luterano*—came to be applied as a term of abuse in the seventeenth century).[2] In the main these characteristics relate to vocabulary and syntax. Another important aspect of Góngora's poetry is its *conceptismo*

[1] *Discorsi del poema eroico*, II, in Torquato Tasso, *Prose*, ed. E. Mazzali (Milan, 1959), p. 529. My translation. See also the interesting note 1 on that page. 'Intelligible' here means 'perceptible to the mind'.

[2] Dámaso Alonso, *Góngora y el 'Polifemo'* (Madrid, 1961), I, 70.

(or *agudeza*, or wit, to use seventeenth-century terms).[1] *Conceptismo*, the use of conceits (*conceptos*), defies rigorous definition. Even Gracián, whose *Agudeza y arte de ingenio* (1648) is a manual of wit, was unable to arrive at a definition that would clearly distinguish a conceit from ordinary metaphors and similes. He wrote: 'Consiste, pues, este artificio conceptuoso en una primorosa concordancia, en una armónica correlación entre dos o tres conoscibles extremos, expresada por un acto del entendimiento... De suerte que se puede definir el concepto. Es un acto del entendimiento que exprime la correspondencia que se halla entre las cosas' (*Discurso*, II). Ordinary tropes could well be included in this definition. The statement has its value, all the same, in emphasising the role of the intellect. Conceits were not aimed at communicating sense-impressions, but at establishing conceptual relationships perceptible to the intellect. To the seventeenth-century mind the more extreme the terms thus related, the more satisfying was the result. Johnson wrote of English Metaphysical poetry: 'But Wit...may be more rigorously and philosophically considered as a kind of *discordia concors*; a combination of dissimilar images, or discovery of occult resemblances in things apparently unlike' (*Life of Abraham Cowley*). So far as it goes, this is accurately observed. The basis of the *conceptista* style, then, is the exploitation of unexpected analogy.

The simplest conceit could be a joke of a quite trivial kind; at the other end of the spectrum, however, a conceit could offer, through a dazzling flash of cross-reference, an enormous compression of meaning, as in this example from a Shakespeare sonnet (urging Mr W. H. to marry and beget children):

> For where is she whose unear'd womb
> Disdains the tillage of thy husbandry? (Sonnet III)

From the pun on 'husbandry'—'playing the part of a husbandman, a farmer' and 'being a husband'—long vistas of meaning open before the reader. Góngora's poetry abounds in conceits,

[1] *Ibid.* pp. 71–83. See also A. A. Parker, 'La agudeza en algunos sonetos de Quevedo', *Estudios dedicados a Menéndez-Pidal*, III (Madrid, 1952), 345–60; and E. L. Rivers, 'El conceptismo del *Polifemo*', *Atenea*, tomo CXLII (Concepción, Chile, July–Sept. 1961), pp. 102–9.

some trivial, some as moving as this epitaph on Doña María de Lira of Toledo:

> La bella Lira muda yace ahora
> debajo deste mármol que, sin duda,
> le ha convocado muda,
> como solía canora:
> si el Tajo arenas dora,
> ilustres piedras; culto monumento
> a este de las Musas instrumento. (Millé, 408)

This Lyre, that in life could move stones as Orpheus did with the music of his lyre, has even in the silence of death the power to draw a stone: the stone that marks her tomb.

One of the effects intended by the *conceptista* writer was that called *admiratio* by the literary theorists of the sixteenth and seventeenth centuries.[1] Unless a stroke of wit caused wonder and surprise in the reader it had failed to that extent in its purpose. A surprising effect is not repeatable; the search for further surprise became in lesser writers a restless pursuit of novelty that often led straight to the trivial and ludicrous. Góngora did not disdain to surprise, as for example when he compares a stream descending to the sea to a moth fluttering into a flame:

> Éntrase el mar por un arroyo breve
> que a recibillo con sediento paso
> de su roca natal se precipita,
> y mucha sal no sólo en poco vaso,
> mas su rüina bebe,
> y su fin, cristalina mariposa
> — no alada, sino undosa —,
> en el farol de Tetis solicita. (*Soledad* II, 1–8)

But one of the marvels of Góngora's poetry is its combination of inventiveness and poise, so that the result is never trivial. No wonder he was so much admired by the fastidious Gracián, who wrote of him: 'Fue este culto poeta cisne en los concentos, águila en los conceptos; en toda especie de agudeza eminente...' (*Agudeza*, Discurso V).

In spite of his fertility in invention there were images and

[1] See E. C. Riley, 'Aspectos del concepto de "Admiratio" en la teoría literaria del Siglo de Oro', *Homenaje a Dámaso Alonso*, III (Madrid, 1963), 173–83.

ideas that he evidently treasured in his mind, since they recur in many different poems over a considerable period of time. Some of the images in the *Soledades* have an ancestry going back twenty years. It is evident that for Góngora they held some special richness of meaning and beauty. An interesting example of how he reused and rewrote can be found in the three sonnets (Millé, 318–20) he composed in 1611 for the *túmulo* or catafalque erected in Córdoba on the death of the queen, Margarita de Austria. The order of composition cannot be determined; the way in which Góngora modified and reused certain images suggests that it is the order in which they appear in the Chacón manuscript, followed in this by the Millé edition. At all events, the three sonnets give us some insight into Góngora's imagination at work.

In the first, several ideas are developed: great estate is a gulf full of reefs, a shore of sirens; many have been wrecked, few have learned prudence. The *túmulo* of Margarita, a pearl (the Greek word from which the name is derived means 'pearl') from the *concha de Baviera* (her birthplace), is a lesson in *desengaño*.

The second picks up and develops the last idea. The *túmulo*, bright with burning candles, exceeds the splendour of the peacock's unfurled tail, but it is a *seña no vana de nuestra vanidad*—unlike the peacock's tail, a symbol of vanity.

The third sonnet is the most poised and successful. The first lacks the rigorous unity Góngora evidently desired. The second develops a unified conceit but fails through its excessive difficulty (it is one of Góngora's most impenetrable poems). The third sonnet follows a unified scheme announced in the first quatrain. The *túmulo* is an unmoved symbol of mutability. It is also a pyre for one who is more glorious than the Phoenix. From the second sonnet is borrowed the reference to burning candles, and from the first the reference to the sea. They are combined in the image of the ship around whose masts plays St Elmo's fire. The instability symbolised by the ship is balanced by the assurance represented by the candle-flames, *hijas de otra mejor Leda*—Mary. A new image enters: the *túmulo* now becomes a lighthouse announcing a safe haven. Finally, it is a shell in which rests Margarita who, a pearl in name, a ruby in charity (whose colour is red) and a diamond in faith (white)—the latter ideas borrowed from the second sonnet—, will rise reborn from the *obscura concha* of death (here represented by the *túmulo*):

renace en nuevo Sol, en nuevo Oriente.

The sonnet can be set out schematically as follows:

The *túmulo*, an unmoving symbol of mutability, A
is the pyre (suggested by the candles) of a better Phoenix. B
It is like a ship assured of divine favour by
St Elmo's fire; its lights make it,
through a paradox, into a lighthouse beckoning to harbour.
Hence it stands for both stillness and movement. A1
It is a shell from which the Queen will be reborn into
a new life (like the Phoenix from its pyre). B1

The unity of the poem is complete. To study it in relation to its two companions tells much about Góngora's untiring devotion to perfection.

Góngora's poetry, then, achieved through its very artifice a richness and variety which it would not be easy to match in seventeenth-century Europe. Conceit, image, rhythm and sound contribute to the effect, as may be judged from the following passage:

Aquél, las ondas escarchando, vuela;
éste, con perezoso movimiento,
el mar encuentra, cuya espuma cana
su parda aguda prora
resplandeciente cuello
hace de augusta Coya peruana,
a quien hilos el Sur tributó ciento
de perlas cada hora.
Lágrimas no enjugó más de la Aurora
sobre víolas negras la mañana,
que arrolló su espolón con pompa vana
caduco aljófar, pero aljófar bello.

Dando el huésped licencia para ello,
recurren no a las redes que, mayores,
mucho Océano y pocas aguas prenden,
sino a las que ambiciosas menos penden,
laberinto nudoso de marino

Dédalo, si de leño no, de lino,
fábrica escrupulosa, y aunque incierta,
siempre murada, pero siempre abierta.

(*Soledad* II, 61–80)

The youth whose wanderings the poem records boards the smaller of two boats, while his companions embark in the larger. The latter flies swiftly over the waves, but the smaller boat goes slowly, butting the waves, which fling spray over its bows. The rhythm of the lines conveys the difference in speed. In line 61, Góngora suggests speed by placing the main stress on the eighth syllable, so that the line seems to rush along precipitately:

Aquél, las ondas escarch**an**do, vuela.

By contrast, the movement of the other boat is expressed by the unhurried rhythm of the next line, which carries over into 63, only to be pulled up short by the stressed *en***cuen***tra*, whose abruptness imitates the boat butting the waves.

Over the boat's prow the sea flings a shower of spray, which Góngora compares with the pearls gathered from the Pacific (*Mar del Sur*) and made into necklaces to adorn the neck of an Inca princess. Góngora puts it more allusively and tellingly: 'Whose spray made of the slender, dusky prow a glittering neck of an august Peruvian princess, to whom the South rendered up every hour a hundred pearls.' The difficulty of the lines lies in their allusiveness, but in their allusiveness and economy lies too their poetic force. To see the sharp prow of a humble fishing boat as like the slender neck of a Peruvian princess shows (to say the least) an imagination of unusual vividness at work.

Góngora now brings in a different image: having compared the splendour of the spray with that of pearls, he compares its shortlived beauty with that of dew: 'Morning did not wipe away more tears from the eyes of Dawn on dark-hued violets than did the boat's prow throw up drops of spray, like shortlived but beautiful pearls.' The first image emphasised the splendour of the sight, this one emphasises its transience. In their sharply etched beauty both images can be enjoyed as poetry, even though their full thematic implications cannot be grasped in isolation from the rest of the poem.

The fishermen now cast their nets, with their guest's permission. The nets are not 'those larger nets that embrace a great expanse of sea, though little water, but of that less ambitious kind that hang deep down, forming a labyrinth—as if contrived by some marine Daedalus—not of wood but string (*lino*)...'. Góngora contrasts here two kinds of fishing. In one, the nets are cast wide, then slowly hauled in, embracing much ocean but little water because the water pours out through their mesh. In the other—known as *trasmallo*—the nets are weighted and sunk vertically to form a trap, a labyrinth from which the fish cannot escape. In its evocative alliteration and in its sinuous pattern of sound, the line *Dédalo, si de leño no, de lino* suggests both the soft lapping of water and the form of the labyrinth itself.

Góngora's poetry, then, works at many levels, and it needs to be read with unusual alertness if all the elements are to fuse into one poetic experience. Góngora demands a lot of his reader, but at the same time offers him great rewards.

## 3 THEMES

Góngora wrote on many subjects, but two themes stand out: transience and mutability in human affairs; and the permanence and beauty of Nature. The two themes are intimately related.

The passage of time was a common subject among sixteenth- and seventeenth-century poets. There is no doubt that it was to some extent a purely conventional subject, an accepted topic; all the same, if we take the literature of the time at its face value as evidence, the transience of life and the approach of death would seem to have had a special poignancy for Góngora's generation and for seventeenth-century Europe in general. The theme appears in Góngora's earliest poetry. It is, for example, the subject of a sonnet written in 1582, *Mientras por competir con tu belleza*. The poetic injunction to a young girl to enjoy her youth and beauty while they last—Ausonius' *collige, virgo, rosas*—was a stock subject for imitation in the Renaissance. It is a commonplace to compare Góngora's sonnet with Garcilaso's on the same theme, *En tanto que de rosa y azucena*. Góngora's sonnet is different from its models, however: it warns not of the coming of old age but of extinction.

Garcilaso's sonnet retains its luminous poise and measure to the end; the last line of Góngora's is a personal cry of horror at the thought of ceasing to exist. Another sonnet written late in life, *Menos solicitó veloz saeta* (1623), warns of the silent passage of time, that wears away the days and gnaws away the years. Between these poems, Góngora wrote many others on the theme. His *romance Esperando están la rosa* ('Del palacio de la primavera', 1609), a hymn to the beauty of the flowers, ends abruptly with the lines:

Las flores a las personas
ciertos ejemplos les den:
que puede ser yermo hoy
el que fue jardín ayer.

In a *letrilla* of 1621 flowers again represent the brevity of life; a marigold laments the passing of its beauty:

*Aprended, Flores, de mí*
*lo que va de ayer a hoy,*
*que ayer maravilla fui,*
*y hoy sombra mía aun no soy.*

A *romance* of 1582 is superficially more lighthearted than the sonnet *Mientras por competir* of that year, but its advice—*carpe diem*—is the same:

Por eso, mozuelas locas,
antes que la edad avara
el rubio cabello de oro
convierta en luciente plata,
quered cuando sois queridas,
amad cuando sois amadas;
mirad, bobas, que detrás
se pinta la ocasión calva.
*¡Que se nos va la Pascua, mozas,*
*que se nos va la Pascua!*

Góngora had plenty of opportunity of studying the mutability of human affairs in the disappointments of his last years at Court, to which he had come with such lively hopes of advancement. In one terrible year he learned a sharper lesson about the uncertainty of life: in October 1621 his friend and protector Rodrigo Calderón was executed, and in August 1622 his friend and fellow-poet, Juan de Tasis, Conde de Villamediana, was murdered by an unknown assailant. Góngora's shock and grief may be read in poems and letters of that time. But the lesson was not a new one and, as I have said, the subject was in any case a literary commonplace. It may not be fanciful to see the theme in some of Góngora's beautiful *romances* on separated lovers, for example that of 1580:

> La más bella niña
> de nuestro lugar,
> hoy viuda y sola
> y ayer por casar.

Equally beautiful examples are the *romances Amarrado al duro banco* (1583) and *Lloraba la niña* (1590).

For Góngora the poetic refuge from the evils and vicissitudes of the Court was Nature: a highly idealised Nature (it goes without saying) deriving from the Renaissance pastoral tradition. I hope to show later in discussing the *Soledades* that Góngora found in a more philosophical contemplation of Nature, the abode and expression of permanence, an answer to the vicissitudes of life itself. The strength of Góngora's attachment to Nature draws life from the strength of his awareness of transience. (Perhaps I may be permitted to put on one side for a moment the apparent contradiction that he uses flowers in some poems as a symbol of mutability.)

One of the poems in which Court and country are brought face to face is the *romance En un pastoral albergue* (1602), based on an episode in Ariosto's *Orlando Furioso*. Imitating the manner of the traditional Spanish ballad, Góngora begins (and ends) abruptly. The time is Charlemagne's. Angelica, the wandering princess of Cathay who has created havoc in Christian Europe by her beauty and coldness, comes upon the body of the young Saracen Medoro, left for dead after a Christian ambush. She falls in love with him and, when restored, he with her. They live a brief idyll in a woodman's cottage and the surrounding country, and depart in time to escape the jealous fury of Orlando, who will lay waste the scene in the madness that overcomes him.

The story is a simple one, but Góngora's treatment of it is not. Though not as difficult as the long poems of 1612–13, the *romance* is full of Góngora's characteristic figures and conceits.[1] Some demand a knowledge of Ariosto's poem (something that Góngora

[1] See Dámaso Alonso, *La lengua poética de Góngora* (Madrid, 1950), 20–37; and E. M. Wilson, 'On Góngora's *Angélica y Medoro*', *Bulletin of Hispanic Studies*, xxx (Liverpool, 1953), 85–94. There is an excellent edition by Dámaso Alonso, *Romance de Angélica y Medoro* (1962).

could take for granted), as when we read of Angelica's discovery of the wounded Medoro, his veins almost empty of blood:

> Las venas con poca sangre,
> los ojos con mucha noche
> le halló en el campo aquella
> vida y muerte de los hombres.

Only previous knowledge explains the reference to Angelica: she is the life of men when she inspires love and a hope that it will be requited, she is their death by her coldness.

On other occasions, Góngora's characteristic metaphors are at first hard to penetrate. For example:

> Límpiale el rostro, y la mano
> siente al Amor que se esconde
> tras las rosas, que la muerte
> va violando sus colores.
> Escondióse tras las rosas
> porque labren sus arpones
> el diamante del Catay
> con aquella sangre noble.

As Angelica wipes away the blood from his face, she falls in love with what she sees, as if stung by Love lurking behind the roses of his cheeks. Love's darts pierce her the more easily because she is already moved by the sight of Medoro's blood: as if Love were cutting a diamond (an allusion to her previous hard-heartedness) softened with blood (a reference to an old belief that diamonds could be softened thus).

The poem presents Nature as a refuge from the two evils of courtly life and war. Medoro, once a warrior, now lays aside his arms and Angelica, a princess, her jewels. They belong now to the country, the home of greater virtue than the Court can boast, as the woodman's pity shows:

> y la que mejor se halla
> en las selvas que en la Corte,
> simple bondad al pío ruego
> cortésmente corresponde.

Here in the country gentle breezes take the place of the flattering tongues of the Court. Nature offers the lovers its bounty, more beautiful than the luxuries of the Court:

> Los campos les dan alfombras,
> los árboles pabellones,
> la apacible fuente sueño,
> música los ruiseñores.

Angelica's acceptance of love and the values of nature is indicated with characteristic obliqueness. Early in the poem she is referred to as *el diamante del Catay*: she is, after all, a princess, and an unloving one at that. Her heart is a flint, so that when mingled pity and love move her to weep at the sight of Medoro her tears are described as *centellas de agua*. After the change wrought in her by love and nature, however:

> Desnuda el pecho anda ella,
> vuela el cabello sin orden;
> si le abrocha, es con claveles,
> con jazmines si le coge.

Medoro was associated at the start of the poem with flowers. Now Angelica, no longer a *diamante*, wears flowers instead of clasps and brooches, badges of artifice.

But danger threatens. The lovers escape in time, but as for the idyllic setting:

> Choza, pues, tálamo y lecho,
> cortesanos labradores,
> aires, campos, fuentes, vegas,
> cuevas, troncos, aves, flores,
> fresnos, chopos, montes, valles,
> contestes de estos amores,
> el Cielo os guarde, si puede,
> de las locuras del Conde.

*Si puede*: but it cannot: Orlando will lay all waste. Góngora introduces thus, with the skill of genius, a quiet comment on the precariousness of human happiness. But the poem is not, after all, entirely a pessimistic one: if Góngora expects us to know from Ariosto the antecedents of the action he must equally expect us to remember the sequel: Angelica and Medoro will reign happily in Cathay, where Orlando cannot reach them. Furthermore, Orlando can hurt but cannot destroy Nature. What, after all, is transitory is Count Orlando and his kind. The poem, with its quiet allusion to what is to come, is 'open-ended' and invites the reader to glance down the vistas it opens.

Góngora's satirical and burlesque poems constitute another important aspect of his work. The satire needs no special analysis: in it Góngora brings his wit to bear on easily identified targets—greed, injustice, etc. These poems are sometimes linguistically difficult but they present no psychological difficulties. This is not the case with all the burlesque poems. Two of these, in particular, are at first somewhat disturbing: the *romances* on Hero and Leander (in two parts, 1589 and 1610; Millé, 27 and 64) and on Pyramus and Thisbe (1618; Millé, 74).[1] These *romances* are comic masterpieces; what makes them disturbing is that Góngora, author of so many exquisite poems on love, here brings all the resources of his wit to the task of mocking two of the most famous of love stories, and mocking them with relish and extraordinary inventiveness in the creation of absurd imagery. Góngora's attitude to the lovers is explicit in both cases. The epitaph of Hero and Leander begins:

> Hero somos y Leandro,
> no menos necios que ilustres...

When Pyramus kills himself, Góngora exclaims:

> ¡Oh, tantas veces insulso,
> cuantas vueltas a tu yerro
> los siglos darán futuros!
> ¿Tan mal te olía la vida?

Is Góngora's target the folly of useless ideals? Probably: it is interesting to note that both pairs of lovers appear in consecutive stanzas in a *letrilla* of 1581 whose refrain expresses a picaresque contempt of the grandiose and self-important:

> *Ándeme yo caliente*
> *y ríase la gente.*

This is the selfsame Góngora who wrote the serious pastoral poetry of the *Soledades*. In the *Soledades* he turns away from the pomp and cares of courtly life to praise the humble, ambitionless

[1] See C. de Salazar Mardones, *Ilustración de la Fábula de Píramo y Tisbe* (1636) or the extracts from it in Góngora, *Píramo y Tisbe*..., por A. Rumeau (Paris, 1961). See also R. Jammes, 'Notes sur la "Fábula de Píramo y Tisbe" de Góngora', *Les Langues Néo-Latines* (Jan. 1961), pp. 1–47; A. Terry, 'An Interpretation of Góngora's *Fábula de Píramo y Tisbe*', *Bulletin of Hispanic Studies* (1956), pp. 202–17; Pamela Waley, 'Enfoque y medios humorísticos de la "Fábula de Píramo y Tisbe"', *Revista de Filología Española*, tomo XLIV (1961), 385–98.

but happy life of goatherds and fishermen. In the *letrilla* he mocks at pomp and riches. Hero and Leander, Pyramus and Thisbe can act out their noble but destructive love; Góngora, in this poetic persona, prefers a jug of wine and a pasty:

Pase a media noche el mar,
y arda en amorosa llama
Leandro por ver su Dama;
que yo más quiero pasar
del golfo de mi lagar
la blanca o roja corriente,
*y ríase la gente.*
Pues Amor es tan cruel,
que de Píramo y su amada
hace tálamo una espada,
do se junten ella y él,
sea mi Tisbe un pastel,
y la espada sea mi diente,
*y ríase la gente.*

I think that here we have the sense of the *romances* in which these lovers are mocked. Throughout his career as a poet Góngora remained true to a vision of life that found value only in the natural and the humble, and saw in vanity, self-importance and useless heroics objects fit only for ridicule. To bear this in mind will help us to determine Góngora's attitude to his courtly and lovesick *peregrino* in the *Soledades*.[1]

## 4 THE 'SOLEDADES'

The first *Soledad* and the *Polifemo* were written by 11 May 1613: on that date Góngora sent them from Córdoba to his friend Pedro de Valencia in Madrid for his opinion. It is not known precisely when the second *Soledad* was written. Pedro de Valencia, an important and influential humanist and an intelligent critic whose opinion was evidently much valued by Góngora, replied in a long letter in June 1613, in which he praises Góngora highly, speaking of 'el amor y respeto con que mucho tiempo ha estimo la persona y ingenio y todas las cosas de V.m., juzgando de sus

[1] I am not forgetting the ode *De la toma de Larache* (1612) and the poems addressed to noblemen, such as the sycophantic *Panegírico al Duque de Lerma* (1617). In these poems Góngora is not often at his best. His heart evidently wasn't in the job.

poesías que se aventajan con grande exceso a todo lo mejor que he leído de griegos y latinos en aquel género...' (Millé, 126 *bis*). He was not uniformly flattering, however: he objected strongly to some of the poet's favourite words and tricks of style (*peinar*, *purpúreo*, *si bien*), as well as to some of the more daring images in particular passages. All the passages objected to were either emended or cut out by Góngora.[1]

According to the seventeenth-century commentators the *Soledades* were to have been four in number, but there was disagreement about their subject. According to Pellicer, it was to have been the four ages of man; but according to Díaz de Rivas: 'La primera *Soledad* se intitula la *Soledad* de los campos...La segunda, la *Soledad* de las riberas; la tercera, la *Soledad* de las selvas, y la cuarta la *Soledad* del yermo....'[2] The second account fits the poem better and is now the generally received opinion. However that may be, Góngora completed only the first *Soledad*, though it can be assumed that the second was not far off completion. As far as is known, the third and fourth were never begun.

The poem is written in *silvas*, a free combination of seven- and eleven-syllable lines not arranged in stanzas and with no fixed rhyme-scheme.

The *Soledades* concern a lovesick youth who, shipwrecked and cast ashore on a plank, makes his way through the countryside, attends a village wedding, stays briefly with an old fisherman and his family and then goes on his way again, at which point the work breaks off. On the face of it, the poem is lacking in unity: the figure of the wanderer is too shadowy and marginal for his story to be regarded as the centre of interest. The poem may seem to dissolve, in fact, into a multitude of lyric fragments. If a distinction is made, however, between 'plot' and 'theme', the wanderer is seen then as merely one element in the development of the poem's theme, which is the richness and permanence of Nature. The lyric imagery is the expression of this underlying theme, constantly present even when Góngora seems at his least relevant.

In the letter quoted earlier (p. 5), Góngora in his defence of the *Soledades* makes some obscure but important claims. He writes

[1] Dámaso Alonso, *Góngora y el 'Polifemo'*, p. 63.
[2] *Soledades*, ed. Dámaso Alonso, p. 9.

approvingly of the difficulty of Ovid's style because it provokes reflection, and claims the same merit for the obscurity of his own poetry: 'eso mismo hallará V.m. en mis "Soledades", si tiene capacidad para quitar la corteza y descubrir lo misterioso que encubren'. In itself this remark may not be of much significance: Góngora may simply be claiming (as he did earlier in the same letter) that his difficult language can be rationally construed. All the same, it must be noted that *corteza* had a precise sense in traditional literary and exegetic terminology: the *cortex* of a text was its surface meaning, within which lay hidden the *nucleus*, its real meaning.[1] Later in the same letter Góngora goes on: 'descubierto lo que está debajo de esos tropos, por fuerza el entendimiento ha de quedar convencido, y convencido, satisfecho: demás que, como el fin de el entendimiento es hacer presa en verdades, que por eso no le satisface nada, si no es la primera verdad, conforme a aquella sentencia de san Agustín: "Inquietum est cor nostrum, donec requiescat in te", en tanto quedará más deleitado, cuanto, obligándole a la especulación por la obscuridad de la obra, fuera hallando debajo de las sombras de la obscuridad, asimilaciones a su concepto'. Góngora's justification of his obscurity is itself somewhat obscure, but he seems to point to some general theme lying behind the profusion of incident and image in the poem. 'Asimilaciones a su concepto' are (as I have suggested) to be interpreted as 'asimilaciones [resemblances or approximations] al concepto de la primera verdad'. Góngora seems to be claiming that in puzzling over the images, allusions and tropes of the *Soledades* the mind is led to an understanding of the source of truth, *la primera verdad*.

The first *Soledad* opens in Spring, when the sun is in Taurus. A youth is cast ashore on a plank.

> De el siempre en la montaña opuesto pino
> al enemigo Noto,
> piadoso miembro roto
> — breve tabla — delfín no fue pequeño
> al inconsiderado peregrino
> que a una Libia de ondas su camino
> fio, y su vida a un leño. (I, 15–20)

[1] See D. W. Robertson, Jr., 'Some Medieval Literary Terminology with Special Reference to Chrétien de Troyes', *Studies in Philology*, XLVIII (1951), 669–92.

*Inconsiderado*: the youth should not have ventured on the sea in the first place. Its profit is illusory: it is a waste place, a *Libia de ondas*.

> Del Océano, pues, antes sorbido,
> y luego vomitado. (I, 22–3)

The sea swallowed him as the whale swallowed Jonah and has now cast him up. Some parallel between the youth and Jonah is shown by *vomitado* (the Vulgate has *evomuit*). Bearing in mind the traditional interpretation of the story of Jonah we are led to assume that the youth is cast up disillusioned with his past life; previously sunk in error, he is now on firm ground.[1] The youth scales a cliff with difficulty and, leaving turbulence and confusion behind him, makes for a distant light. It is the

> farol de una cabaña
> que sobre el ferro está, en aquel incierto
> golfo de sombras, anunciando el puerto. (I, 59–61)

In the darkness of confusion or error it is the light of a port which, unlike the youth, is firmly anchored. If the opening of the poem is in fact allegorical, the allegory ends here; from now on life itself is to offer the youth its moral lessons.

He is welcomed by goatherds, humbly obedient to Nature's laws, and given by them a meal which he eats off a table described as *cuadrado pino*, suggesting, if we bear in mind the *pino* of the ship (I, 15), a contrast between a legitimate and an illegitimate use of Nature. Greed prompts man to make ships and to venture on the sea, an alien element; these goatherds make an innocent use of Nature's gifts. Shipwreck has shown the disastrous consequences of perverting Nature.

The youth sleeps on skins and is awakened by dogs, not the drums of war. Next morning he surveys the countryside and is shown a castle:

> Aquellas que los árboles apenas
> dejan ser torres hoy — dijo el cabrero
> con muestras de dolor extraordinarias —

[1] The opening of *Soledad* I is pretty clearly a version of a widespread topic. See R. O. Jones, 'The Poetic Unity of the *Soledades* of Góngora', *Bulletin of Hispanic Studies*, XXXI (1954), 189–204.

las estrellas nocturnas luminarias
  eran de sus almenas,
cuando, el que ves sayal, fue limpio acero.
Yacen ahora, y sus desnudas piedras
  visten piadosas yedras:
  que a rüinas y a estragos,
sabe el tiempo hacer verdes halagos. (I, 212–21)

Part of the underlying theme of the poem is the vanity of opposing Nature, which destroys artifice and punishes presumption. Only Nature itself is immutable. This theme irrupts into the poem in image after image that are, as here, superficially irrelevant to the wanderer's journey. The picture of trees overshadowing once proud towers and of ivy clothing the ruined walls is clearly symbolic. Like many other examples in the poem, it is a verbal counterpart of the emblems—allegorical pictures embodying a maxim or moral—so popular at the time.

The mouldering castle is in contrast with the river of I, 197–211, which represents the bounty and the permanence of Nature. The juxtaposition is significant: war makes sterile, peace makes fertile. The war–peace antithesis is part of the poem's theme.

The youth joins a party bearing gifts to a marriage feast. The gifts are common birds and beasts, but all described in terms of exotic splendour: coral, gold, mother-of-pearl, sapphires, rubies. The point seems clear: this is the wealth of Nature, better than all the illusory riches of the Indies.

As the procession rests, an old man addresses to the youth a denunciation of seafaring (I, 366–502). The opening lines depict the first mariner as not only unnatural but futile. His natural element was the earth—*labrador*—but he transferred his labour to the sea, where his work was in vain—*surcó...el campo undoso*, where ploughing is profitless (recalling the *Libia de ondas*). The perversion of Nature—*mal nacido pino*—brings only disaster: not merely shipwreck but, as the reference to the Trojan horse shows (I, 374–8), discord and war. Seafaring impelled by greed is not only debased but finally profitless: a moral order is broken together with the physical one and only disaster can follow. The idea was not a new one, but the form given it by Góngora is original, and deeply felt.

The speech culminates in the superb lines on the Spice Islands.

> De firmes islas no la inmóvil flota
> en aquel Mar del Alba te describo,
> cuyo número — ya que no lascivo —
> por lo bello agradable y por lo vario
> la dulce confusión hacer podía,
> que en los blancos estanques del Eurota
> la virginal desnuda montería,
> haciendo escollos o de mármol pario
> o de terso marfil sus miembros bellos,
> que pudo bien Acteón perderse en ellos. (I, 481–90)

The lines express the intoxication with beauty of the first Europeans to see the islands, which dazzle the mind as much as the sight of Diana and her maidens bathing naked dazzled Actaeon's.[1] The implications are worth unravelling. The islands are virginal, like Diana, because they are as yet unpillaged. Actaeon was turned into a wild beast for his curiosity and was hunted to death by his own dogs. Góngora implies that discoveries inspired by greed destroy the discoverers. So, although the lines convey all the ravishment of the senses felt by the voyagers, Góngora adds—with characteristic obliquity—a final condemnation of their daring.

The procession takes up its burdens again (*cual próvidas hormigas*, in prudent contrast to the folly of mariners) and makes its way singing through a grove where

> Pintadas aves — cítaras de pluma —
> coronaban la bárbara capilla. (I, 556–7)

The grove is a natural temple whose organ—*cítara*—is birdsong and whose congregation is the listening stream.

At the wedding a hymn to Hymen invokes fertility for the marriage. The bride emerges, accompanied by her attendants,

> cual nueva fénix en flamantes plumas
> matutinos del sol rayos vestida,
> de cuanta surca el aire acompañada

[1] Góngora may have drawn on Lupercio Leonardo de Argensola's *Conquista de las Islas Molucas* (Madrid, 1609), in which the account of the discovery is based ultimately on the description by Pigafetta, who sailed with Magellan. Argensola's account of the continuous strife which ravaged the islands in the sixteenth and seventeenth centuries adds point to Góngora's lines. Unless the historical background to Góngora's poetry is borne in mind, the poetry loses much of its point. Góngora lived in a time when Spanish confidence was on the wane, when intelligent men were aware of the enormous social, economic and political problems facing Spain.

monarquía canora;
y, vadeando nubes, las espumas
del rey corona de los otros ríos;
en cuya orilla el viento hereda ahora
pequeños no vacíos
de funerales bárbaros trofeos
que el Egipto erigió a sus Ptolomeos. (I, 948–57)

This simile has an emblematic compactness. The bride is like the Phoenix because the bird has just been reborn; so has the girl, into a new kind of life—she was described in the chorus to Hymen as *en los inciertos de su edad segunda crepúsculos*. The Phoenix is immortal though it suffers an apparent death; the girl will achieve a kind of immortality in her children. Both are fulfilled in the natural process of death and rebirth. Góngora goes on now to describe the windy spaces where the Pyramids, symbols of death and monuments to vanity, once stood (he believed them to have since disappeared, as Salcedo Coronel makes clear in his commentary). A perfect contrast is established, therefore, between the constantly reborn vitality of Nature and of those who submit to her laws, and the inevitable decay of those who attempt to defy her. The Pyramids stood on the banks of the Nile, an ancient symbol of fertility. This must recall the castle mouldering on the banks of another life-giving river earlier in the poem. This simile, then, sums up an important part of the theme of the poem: the contrast between the beauty, innocence and fertility of Nature and the ultimate futility of whatever opposes her.

In the second *Soledad* the wanderer joins some poor fishermen. The fishers gather their own food but they feed richly, like kings and consuls. Góngora holds up their way of life for admiration; clearly we are not to think of them as breaking the natural order by venturing on the sea, since they are impelled not by greed but by honest necessity and since they do not trade but gather the freely given fruits of Nature. (When the youth sits down to a meal at their cottage, they eat fish—*raros muchos, y todos no comprados* (II, 247). A prosaic detail!)

The old fisherman and his family exemplify once again the innocence of those obedient to Nature. Everything around them speaks its lesson. The wanderer sees their swans.

> En la más seca, en la más limpia anea
> vivificando están muchos sus huevos,
> y mientras dulce aquél su muerte anuncia
> entre la verde juncia,
> sus pollos éste al mar conduce nuevos. (II, 255–9)

Like the Phoenix, these birds represent the continual replenishment and vitality of Nature in whom, though death is inescapable, life ultimately prevails. (Flowers can therefore without contradiction be used by Góngora as symbols of transience: each bloom will die, but flowers will continue to bloom.) Everything in the garden plays its symbolic part: doves are emblematic of love and innocence; rabbits, of fertility and rustic unwarlikeness; bees, of industry and the bounty of Nature. The queen bee is a

> susurrante amazona, Dido alada,
> de ejército más casto, de más bella
> república, ceñida, en vez de muros,
> de cortezas; en esta, pues, Cartago
> reina la abeja... (II, 290–4)

She is queen of a better city because Carthage was a commercial city which was finally destroyed through wars provoked by commercial rivalry with Rome. The bee is protected not by walls but bark. Innocence is the best protection, and without innocence all protection is vain.

A word now on the wanderer. In contrast with all around him in both *Soledades* he is immersed in gloom. He is a victim of unhappy love; his thoughts are of death, not life, and the imagery of his thoughts and songs is funereal (e.g. I, 737–42; II, 116–71). This carries its own comment: he is of the breed of Pyramus, and Góngora has made his attitude plain elsewhere. But we need not go outside the *Soledades* for evidence. In II, 651–76, Góngora contrasts the favour shown by Cupid to humble fishermen (whose love is returned) and the disappointment in love that drove the wanderer from palaces

> en que la arquitectura
> a la gëometría se rebela,
> jaspes calzada y pórfidos vestida. (II, 669–71)

The wanderer's wretched state is part and parcel of his courtly past. Love dwells in cottages, not palaces. The parallel with Angelica and Medoro is irresistibly forced on us.[1]

The old fisherman describes in a piscatory eclogue how his daughters hunt the seal and other marine creatures. Two suitors arrive and sing an amœbæan song. Shortly after, the wanderer leaves for the mainland where, in a venatory eclogue, he witnesses a hawking scene. There the poem ends. It is not known why Góngora broke off. Perhaps he had reached the limit of what he could achieve within the strict poetic discipline he had set himself. Perhaps the increasing anxieties of his life—especially after 1617—gave him insufficient leisure.

One or two aspects remain to be commented on. A reader cannot fail to be struck by the many references to music in the poem. Their full force cannot be felt unless we bear in mind the significance of music for Renaissance Europe.

It is not too much to say that for an educated man of the early seventeenth century, music, the idea and the reality—or, more precisely, *musica speculativa* and *musica practica*—carried an inescapable aura of myth, speculation and philosophy. Music and references to it in poetry were a shorthand sign for the harmony of the universe. This preoccupation with harmony pervaded European thought and literature of the Renaissance.[2] The closer one's acquaintance with Renaissance attitudes to music, the stronger must be the conviction that only the most trivial and occasional references to music in Renaissance literature are completely devoid of overtones that held the universe in a shimmering web of harmony.

For Góngora's contemporaries the 'harmony' of the universe had not yet become an empty metaphor; or a metaphor at all, in fact. It is clear from the texts that a real state analogous to music

[1] See, however, A. Vilanova, 'El peregrino de amor en las *Soledades* de Góngora', *Estudios dedicados a Menéndez Pidal*, III (Madrid, 1952), 420–60. In this important study the literary antecedents of the *peregrino de amor* are traced. I cannot accept the author's conclusion that the *Soledades*, if Góngora had gone on with them, would have expressed finally a disillusioned rejection of the world, since it is clear that Góngora puts the melancholy of the wanderer in an unfavourable light and upholds Nature as the only source of value. But no argument, in any case, can be based on the unwritten *Soledades*.

[2] See R. O. Jones, 'Neoplatonism and the *Soledades*', *Bulletin of Hispanic Studies* (1963), pp. 1–16.

is connoted by the word, and of that state audible music is only one manifestation, albeit the aptest to symbolise the whole. These vast implications are present in Góngora.

The concept of the harmony of the universe was an old one, developed by the Neoplatonists of the ancient world from root-ideas in the Pythagoreans and in Plato himself. These ideas were transmitted by Boethius, who in his *De Musica* divided music into three branches: *musica mundana*, *humana* and *instrumentalis*. *Musica mundana* was for him the harmony of the entire universe in all its parts. Writers on music up to the seventeenth century felt obliged to begin with an account of *musica mundana*, the vast symphony that governed the movements of the heavenly bodies, the coupling of the elements, the procession of the seasons, the generation, growth and death of all living creatures.

To approach the references to music in the *Soledades* in the light of this tradition is to find in them echoes of the larger harmonies of the universe. Birds singing in a grove are like an organ sounding in a natural temple (I, 556–61). Another reference, and one of the most beautiful, is this:

> Rompida el agua en las menudas piedras,
> cristalina sonante era tiorba,
> y las confusamente acordes aves,
> entre las verdes roscas de las yedras,
> muchas eran, y muchas veces nueve
> aladas musas, que — de pluma leve
> engañada su oculta lira corva —
> metros inciertos sí, pero süaves,
> en idiomas cantan diferentes. (II, 349–57)

The harmony of Nature is close to the surface here. The lines are an echo of that *musica mundana* which had such a hold on the imagination. They describe the music—usually unperceived—inherent in all the scenes and operations of Nature. The birds are like the Muses, though their harmonies are not easily made out (*confusamente acordes*). The water is a theorbo, always resounding in sympathy with the harmonies about it.

There are many other references to music in the poem, too many to be discussed here in detail. They build up a picture of a harmonious universe whose every part resonates in sympathy with every other. In the very widest sense, the *Soledades* are a poetic notation of that harmony.

This everlasting harmony can contain local discord, violence and decay: the discord is resolved in the overriding harmony of the whole. An individual dies but the species lives on (like the Phoenix and the swans). Góngora's vision of a Nature brimming with life, ruled by a harmony in which all discord is resolved, suggests that his thought had a Neoplatonic cast.[1] True, the core of Neoplatonism—the emanations that radiate from God down, from level to level, through all creation—is absent; what Góngora describes is not the process but the product. But even the process is implicit in the poetry when Góngora alludes to the sympathies that exist between man and Nature, between animate and inanimate: as when a stream listens to *serranas* and birds singing in a grove (I, 550–61), and the sea listens compassionately to the *peregrino*'s song (II, 179–84).[2] However, Neoplatonism is only the background to the *Soledades*: they were not written as a systematic exposition of a philosophy but to express Góngora's joyful awareness of the richness of creation. All the same, to look at the poem in this way is to see that Góngora's claim that it was concerned in some way with *la primera verdad* was not unjustified. The *Soledades* are a hymn to the beauty, innocence and permanence of Nature; but the perceptive reader can catch echoes in the poetry of the harmonies whereby, for Góngora, the fabric of the visible universe is sustained.

[1] The revival of Neoplatonism, a synthesis of elements drawn from many sources, was one of the most important features of the Renaissance. According to the Neoplatonists the universe was a living whole held together in harmony by the love and beauty emanating from God. From Renaissance Neoplatonism derived the impulse to observe and study Nature which led ultimately to the development of modern empirical science. See Nesca A. Robb, *Neoplatonism of the Italian Renaissance* (London, 1935); and for more esoteric aspects, Frances A. Yates, *Giordano Bruno and the Hermetic Tradition* (London, 1964).

[2] Luis de León's, too, was a Neoplatonism without the emanations. See *Pastor* in *De los nombres de Cristo*.

# 5 THE 'FÁBULA DE POLIFEMO Y GALATEA'

The *Fábula de Polifemo y Galatea* is a retelling of the story of Acis and Galatea from Ovid's *Metamorphoses*, XIII.[1] The story is a simple one: it tells how Acis wins the love of Galatea, unsuccessfully wooed by the Cyclops Polyphemus. Enraged with jealousy at Acis' success Polyphemus kills him with a rock. Acis is turned into a stream by the compassionate gods. Ovid's version was widely imitated by poets of the sixteenth and seventeenth centuries. What probably prompted Góngora to write his *Polifemo* was the posthumous publication in 1611 of a *Fábula de Acis y Galatea* by Don Luis Carrillo de Sotomayor. Carrillo dedicated the poem to the Conde de Niebla, to whom Góngora was to dedicate his own version later. Góngora borrowed nothing from Carrillo's poem, a very fine work; but its beauty evidently spurred him to try to rival it. Carrillo, like most other poets who wrote on the subject, followed Ovid very closely; Góngora did not: the freedom of his treatment and the originality of his style allow us to consider his *Polifemo* as a personal creation in every important respect, and to interpret it accordingly.

The *Polifemo* is thematically complex, but it is more compact and less rambling than the *Soledades*: naturally enough, since Góngora has a story to tell and is following a model. The very verse form reflects this: the poem is written in *octavas reales* (eight eleven-syllable lines rhyming *abababcc*), whose rigid strength contrasts with the easy enveloping flow of the *silvas* of the *Soledades*.

The focus of the poem is Galatea and the love she inspires, a love that seems to have the power of a force of Nature. Not only Acis and Polyphemus but all the men of Sicily burn for Galatea, who becomes in the poem almost a goddess of love.

> De cuantos siegan oro, esquilan nieve,
> o en pipas guardan la exprimida grana,
> bien sea religión, bien amor sea,
> deidad, aunque sin templo, es Galatea.

[1] See Dámaso Alonso, *Góngora y el 'Polifemo'*, I, 174–218. See also the very important work by A. Vilanova, *Las fuentes y los temas del Polifemo de Góngora*, 2 vols. (Madrid, 1957).

Sicily is described in terms of abounding fertility, all laid at the feet of Galatea, who seems to preside over love and fertility together. She is a goddess without a temple but:

> Sin aras, no: que el margen donde para
> del espumoso mar su pie ligero,
> al labrador, de sus primicias ara,
> de sus esquilmos es al ganadero;
> de la Copia — a la tierra, poco avara —
> el cuerno vierte el hortelano, entero,
> sobre la mimbre que tejió, prolija,
> si artificiosa no, su honesta hija.

Acis and Galatea together typify love and beauty. Góngora's undetailed description evokes images of the purest Classical beauty. Galatea is put before us with a strongly sensual immediacy, but Góngora's careful lack of detail allows her to embody a universal ideal.

> Purpúreas rosas sobre Galatea
> la Alba entre lilios cándidos deshoja:
> duda el Amor cuál más su color sea,
> o púrpura nevada, o nieve roja.
> De su frente la perla es, eritrea,
> émula vana. El ciego dios se enoja,
> y, condenado su esplendor, la deja
> pender en oro al nácar de su oreja.

Acis is similarly unburdened with detail: Góngora conjures up his slender and beautiful form in a single line:

> Era Acis un venablo de Cupido.

Polyphemus, on the other hand, is a monster: a Cyclops for whom the stoutest pine is a weak staff. In Acis and Galatea, Góngora evokes ideal forms that each reader must embody in an image; Polyphemus—untypical, not a universal that the reader can be left to imagine for himself—needs more detail. Góngora devotes three stanzas to his mountainous size, his single eye, his black hair, his uncombed beard, and his garb. Góngora emphasises by every detail the difference between the hirsute and unbeautiful Cyclops and the figures of the lovers.

In the song of love that Polyphemus addresses to Galatea the two themes of love and fertility appear united again. His wealth—

the wealth of the herder and farmer—associates him with Nature: he too shares in the teeming plenty of Sicily. Indeed, Góngora was careful to associate Polyphemus with the abundance of Nature right from his first appearance in the poem, in stanzas 10 and 11, which describe the fruits carried by the Cyclops in his *zurrón*. Love has tamed the giant's ferocity: in his song he tells how he has come through love to know pity. The initial description of Polyphemus' cave and of the Cyclops himself emphasises the monstrous and alarming: he is the 'horror de aquella sierra'. However, in his love-song, which contains some of Góngora's finest poetry, Polyphemus and his sorrows are humanised and brought close to us. The Cyclops is inhuman in his stature and his ferocity; he is as defenceless as any man, however, against the effects of love. He is an uncouth cousin of Acis.

The love with which all Sicily burns causes normal work to be abandoned as ploughman and shepherd dream of Galatea; it is a love that has the overwhelming power of an elemental natural force. By associating this love with the fertility of the island Góngora presents a picture of mingled harmony (love, fertility) and discord (love's disruptive power). Polyphemus and the men of the island can only aspire to harmony since Galatea rejects them; only Acis achieves it, but to have it broken by death. Must the poem then be interpreted as a pessimistic one in which Góngora paints a picture of brimming love and life only to leave us mourning their extinction?

The *Polifemo* is undoubtedly another of Góngora's poems on the precariousness of human happiness. It offers analogies with the *romance* on Angelica and Medoro. In both poems the lovers enjoy a brief and passionate idyll. Polyphemus brings disaster; Count Orlando will lay waste the scene. Both are blinded by jealousy. Finally, each poem is the remaking of a well-known original. Of course, there are differences, too. Angelica and Medoro will reach Cathay and live on happily there, but Acis is killed: violence plays a more obvious role in the *Polifemo*. However, the analogies are more striking than the differences. Both poems can be reduced to one scheme: a sudden victory of love over disdain; passionate love consummated beneath the threat of violence; jealous revenge.

The analogy must not be forced, but it may help to reveal the unifying mood of the *Polifemo*. It is a poem on the brevity of happiness but, like the *romance*, it is not a pessimistic work. The emphasis throughout is on life and beauty. Love can be a disruptive power but it is still a yearning for harmony. One man's harmony, however, is another's discord: the love of Acis and Galatea breeds the jealousy of Polyphemus. For a moment everything is discord as Acis is killed, but the discord is resolved: Acis is changed into a stream, beautiful in itself and a cause of beauty, and his reception in the arms of the sea culminates in what is distinctly a note of triumph:

> Sus miembros lastimosamente opresos
> del escollo fatal fueron apenas,
> que los pies de los árboles más gruesos
> calzó el líquido aljófar de sus venas.
> Corriente plata al fin sus blancos huesos,
> lamiendo flores y argentando arenas,
> a Doris llega, que, con llanto pío,
> yernó lo saludó, lo aclamó río.

This, then, is a story in which, though death enters, vitality prevails. The action takes place on an island which may be symbolic of human life; but if it is, the sea around it does not symbolise—like Jorge Manrique's sea—any ordinary conception of death since the sea, too, is abounding in life. The sea suggests rather that Nature to which all things return. (Both Acis and Galatea are children of creatures of the sea; whereas Polyphemus' father was Neptune himself.) Perhaps in this poem another echo is caught of Renaissance Neoplatonism, though in too diffuse a form to permit precise formulation. In the *Polifemo*, as in the *Soledades*, Góngora seems to move in a poetic atmosphere of optimism in which death is absorbed into the invincible harmony of the universe. For the Neoplatonist, the universe is wholly good; but the very abundance of created things leads inevitably to conflict between some of them. These apparent discords—violence, the preying of animals one on another, death, decay—are in reality only parts of a larger concert. Plotinus, a great influence on Renaissance thought, put it thus:

'Besides, these accidents are not without their service in the co-ordination and completion of the Universal system. One thing perishes, and the Cosmic Reason—whose control nothing anywhere eludes—employs that ending to the beginning of something new.' Góngora may not have known the *Enneads* or any other Neoplatonic treatise; that does not matter: such ideas were widely diffused by the seventeenth century far beyond the bounds of formal Neoplatonism. It is helpful to recall these ideas since they seem to express the spirit of Góngora's poetry. Perhaps Plotinus can have the last word: imagining the universe as a tree rooted in its creator, he describes the manifold branching out into all the diverse forms of created things, so diverse that at their furthest from the root the branches seem to stand in opposition to each other, though in reality there is no opposition and no conflict in the grand scheme. 'The things that act upon each other are branchings from a far-off beginning and so stand distinct; but they derive initially from the one source: all interaction is like that of brothers, resemblant as drawing life from the same parents.'[1]

## 6 FURTHER READING

Dámaso Alonso, *Estudios y ensayos gongorinos* (Madrid, 1955).
Dámaso Alonso, *La lengua poética de Góngora* (Madrid, 1935; 2nd ed. 1950).
Dámaso Alonso, *Góngora y el 'Polifemo'*, 2 vols. (Madrid, 1961).
M. Artigas, *Don Luis de Góngora y Argote* (Madrid, 1925).
Eunice Joiner Gates, *Documentos gongorinos* (Mexico, 1960).
Antonio Vilanova, *Las fuentes y los temas del Polifemo de Góngora*, 2 vols. (Madrid, 1957).

[1] Plotinus, *Enneads*, trans. Stephen MacKenna (London, 1956), pp. 164–5, 185.

# POEMS

For the *Soledad primera* and the *Fábula de Polifemo* I have followed the texts established by Dámaso Alonso, with one or two small changes of punctuation. For the *letrillas* I have followed Robert Jammes' critical edition of Góngora's *letrillas* (Paris, 1963), and for the other poems I have normally followed the Millé edition. I have modernised spelling where this did not involve a change of pronunciation.

## I 'SOLEDAD PRIMERA' (1613)

*Al Duque de Béjar*

[*Dedication*]

Pasos de un peregrino son errante
cuantos me dictó versos dulce musa:
en soledad confusa
perdidos unos, otros inspirados.

¡Oh tú, que, de venablos impedido 5
— muros de abeto, almenas de diamante —,
bates los montes, que, de nieve armados,
gigantes de cristal los teme el cielo;
donde el cuerno, del eco repetido,
fieras te expone, que — al teñido suelo, 10
muertas, pidiendo términos disformes —
espumoso coral le dan al Tormes!:

arrima a un fresno el fresno — cuyo acero,
sangre sudando, en tiempo hará breve
purpurear la nieve — 15
y, en cuanto da el solícito montero
al duro robre, al pino levantado
— émulos vividores de las peñas —
las formidables señas
del oso que aun besaba, atravesado, 20
la asta de tu luciente jabalina,
— o lo sagrado supla de la encina
lo augusto del dosel; o de la fuente
la alta zanefa, lo majestuoso
del sitïal a tu deidad debido —, 25
¡oh Duque esclarecido!,
templa en sus ondas tu fatiga ardiente,
y, entregados tus miembros al reposo
sobre el de grama césped no desnudo,
déjate un rato hallar del pie acertado 30
que sus errantes pasos ha votado
a la real cadena de tu escudo.

Honre süave, generoso nudo
libertad, de fortuna perseguida:
35 que, a tu piedad Euterpe agradecida,
su canoro dará dulce instrumento,
cuando la Fama no su trompa al viento.

## *Soledad Primera*

Era del año la estación florida
en que el mentido robador de Europa
— media luna las armas de su frente,
y el Sol todos los rayos de su pelo —,
5 luciente honor del cielo,
en campos de zafiro pace estrellas;
cuando el que ministrar podía la copa
a Júpiter mejor que el garzón de Ida,
— náufrago y desdeñado, sobre ausente —
10 lagrimosas de amor dulces querellas
da al mar; que condolido,
fue a las ondas, fue al viento
el mísero gemido,
segundo de Arión dulce instrumento.

15 Del siempre en la montaña opuesto pino
al enemigo Noto,
piadoso miembro roto
— breve tabla — delfín no fue pequeño
al inconsiderado peregrino
20 que a una Libia de ondas su camino
fio, y su vida a un leño.

Del Océano pues antes sorbido,
y luego vomitado
no lejos de un escollo coronado
25 de secos juncos, de calientes plumas,
— alga todo y espumas —
halló hospitalidad donde halló nido
de Júpiter el ave.

Besa la arena, y de la rota nave
        aquella parte poca                                        30
que le expuso en la playa dio a la roca;
        que aun se dejan las peñas
lisonjear de agradecidas señas.

Desnudo el joven, cuanto ya el vestido
        Océano ha bebido,                                        35
restituir le hace a las arenas;
        y al sol lo extiende luego,
        que, lamiéndolo apenas
su dulce lengua de templado fuego,
lento lo embiste, y con süave estilo                             40
la menor onda chupa al menor hilo.

No bien pues de su luz los horizontes
— que hacían desigual, confusamente
montes de agua y piélagos de montes —
        desdorados los siente,                                   45
cuando — entregado el mísero extranjero
en lo que ya del mar redimió fiero —
entre espinas crepúsculos pisando,
riscos que aun igualara mal, volando,
        veloz, intrépida ala,                                    50
—menos cansado que confuso — escala.

        Vencida al fin la cumbre
        — del mar siempre sonante,
        de la muda campaña
árbitro igual e inexpugnable muro —,                             55
        con pie ya más seguro
        declina al vacilante
breve esplendor de mal distinta lumbre:
        farol de una cabaña
que sobre el ferro está, en aquel incierto                       60
golfo de sombras anunciando el puerto.

'Rayos — les dice — ya que no de Leda
trémulos hijos, sed de mi fortuna
término luminoso.' Y — recelando
65 de invidïosa bárbara arboleda
interposición, cuando
de vientos no conjuración alguna —
cual, haciendo el villano
la fragosa montaña fácil llano,
70 atento sigue aquella
— aun a pesar de las tinieblas bella,
aun a pesar de las estrellas clara —
piedra, indigna tiara
— si tradición apócrifa no miente —
75 de animal tenebroso, cuya frente
carro es brillante de nocturno día:
tal, diligente, el paso
el joven apresura,
midiendo la espesura
80 con igual pie que el raso,
fijo — a despecho de la niebla fría —
en el carbunclo, norte de su aguja,
o el Austro brame o la arboleda cruja.

El can ya, vigilante,
85 convoca, despidiendo al caminante;
y la que desviada
luz poca pareció, tanta es vecina,
que yace en ella la robusta encina,
mariposa en cenizas desatada.

90 Llegó pues el mancebo, y saludado,
sin ambición, sin pompa de palabras,
de los conducidores fue de cabras,
que a Vulcano tenían coronado.

¡Oh bienaventurado
95 albergue a cualquier hora,
templo de Pales, alquería de Flora!
No moderno artificio
borró designios, bosquejó modelos,

al cóncavo ajustando de los cielos
el sublime edificio; 100
retamas sobre robre
tu fábrica son pobre,
do guarda, en vez de acero,
la inocencia al cabrero
más que el silbo al ganado. 105
¡Oh bienaventurado
albergue a cualquier hora!

No en ti la ambición mora
hidrópica de viento,
ni la que su alimento 110
el áspid es gitano;
no la que, en vulto comenzando humano,
acaba en mortal fiera,
esfinge bachillera,
que hace hoy a Narciso 115
ecos solicitar, desdeñar fuentes;
ni la que en salvas gasta impertinentes
la pólvora del tiempo más preciso:
ceremonia profana
que la sinceridad burla villana 120
sobre el corvo cayado.
¡Oh bienaventurado
albergue a cualquier hora!

Tus umbrales ignora
la adulación, sirena 125
de reales palacios, cuya arena
besó ya tanto leño:
trofeos dulces de un canoro sueño.
No a la soberbia está aquí la mentira
dorándole los pies, en cuanto gira 130
la esfera de sus plumas,
ni de los rayos baja a las espumas
favor de cera alado.
¡Oh bienaventurado
albergue a cualquier hora! 135

No pues de aquella sierra — engendradora
más de fierezas que de cortesía —
la gente parecía
que hospedó al forastero
140 con pecho igual de aquel candor primero,
que, en las selvas contento,
tienda el fresno le dio, el robre alimento.

Limpio sayal, en vez de blanco lino,
cubrió el cuadrado pino;
145 y en boj, aunque rebelde, a quien el torno
forma elegante dio sin culto adorno,
leche que exprimir vio la Alba aquel día
— mientras perdían con ella
los blancos lilios de su frente bella —,
150 gruesa le dan y fría,
impenetrable casi a la cuchara,
del viejo Alcimedón invención rara.

El que de cabras fue dos veces ciento
esposo casi un lustro — cuyo diente
155 no perdonó a racimo aun en la frente
de Baco, cuanto más en su sarmiento —
(triunfador siempre de celosas lides,
lo coronó el Amor; mas rival tierno,
breve de barba y duro no de cuerno,
160 redimió con su muerte tantas vides)
servido ya en cecina,
purpúreos hilos es de grana fina.

Sobre corchos después, más regalado
sueño le solicitan pieles blandas,
165 que al príncipe entre holandas,
púrpura tiria o milanés brocado.
No de humosos vinos agravado
es Sísifo en la cuesta, si en la cumbre
de ponderosa vana pesadumbre,
170 es, cuanto más despierto, más burlado.

De trompa militar no, o destemplado
son de cajas, fue el sueño interrumpido;
    de can sí, embravecido
    contra la seca hoja
que el viento repeló a alguna coscoja. 175

Durmió, y recuerda al fin, cuando las aves
— esquilas dulces de sonora pluma —
    señas dieron süaves
del alba al sol, que el pabellón de espuma
    dejó, y en su carroza 180
rayó el verde obelisco de la choza.

Agradecido, pues, el peregrino,
deja el albergue y sale acompañado
de quien lo lleva donde, levantado,
distante pocos pasos del camino, 185
imperïoso mira la campaña
un escollo, apacible galería,
que festivo teatro fue algún día
de cuantos pisan faunos la montaña.

    Llegó, y, a vista tanta 190
obedeciendo la dudosa planta,
inmóvil se quedó sobre un lentisco,
verde balcón del agradable risco.

Si mucho poco mapa les despliega,
mucho es más lo que, nieblas desatando, 195
confunde el sol y la distancia niega.
Muda la admiración, habla callando,
y, ciega, un río sigue, que — luciente
    de aquellos montes hijo —
con torcido discurso, aunque prolijo, 200
tiraniza los campos útilmente;
orladas sus orillas de frutales,
quiere la Copia que su cuerno sea
— si al animal armaron de Amaltea
    diáfanos cristales —; 205
engazando edificios en su plata,

de muros se corona,
rocas abraza, islas aprisiona,
de la alta gruta donde se desata
210 hasta los jaspes líquidos, adonde
su orgullo pierde y su memoria esconde.

'Aquéllas que los árboles apenas
dejan ser torres hoy — dijo el cabrero
con muestras de dolor extraordinarias —
215 las estrellas nocturnas luminarias
eran de sus almenas,
cuando el que ves sayal fue limpio acero.
Yacen ahora, y sus desnudas piedras
visten piadosas yedras:
220 que a rüinas y a estragos,
sabe el tiempo hacer verdes halagos.'

Con gusto el joven y atención le oía,
cuando torrente de armas y de perros,
que si precipitados no los cerros,
225 las personas tras de un lobo traía,
tierno discurso y dulce compañía
dejar hizo al serrano,
que — del sublime espacïoso llano
al huésped al camino reduciendo —
230 al venatorio estruendo,
pasos dando veloces,
número crece y multiplica voces.

Bajaba entre sí el joven admirando,
armado a Pan o semicapro a Marte,
235 en el pastor mentidos, que con arte
culto principio dio al discurso, cuando
rémora de sus pasos fue su oído,
dulcemente impedido
de canoro instrumento, que pulsado
240 era de una serrana junto a un tronco,
sobre un arroyo, de quejarse ronco,
mudo sus ondas, cuando no enfrenado.

Otra con ella montaraz zagala
juntaba el cristal líquido al humano
por el arcaduz bello de una mano 245
que al uno menosprecia, al otro iguala.

Del verde margen otra las mejores
rosas traslada y lilios al cabello,
o por lo matizado o por lo bello,
si Aurora no con rayos, Sol con flores. 250

Negras pizarras entre blancos dedos
ingenïosa hiere otra, que dudo
que aun los peñascos la escucharan quedos.
    Al son pues deste rudo
    sonoroso instrumento 255
    — lasciva el movimiento,
    mas los ojos honesta —
altera otra, bailando, la floresta.

Tantas al fin el arroyuelo, y tantas
montañesas da el prado, que dirías 260
ser menos las que verdes Hamadrías
    abortaron las plantas:
    inundación hermosa
que la montaña hizo populosa
    de sus aldeas todas 265
    a pastorales bodas.

    De una encina embebido
en lo cóncavo, el joven mantenía
la vista de hermosura, y el oído
    de métrica armonía. 270
    El Sileno buscaba
de aquellas que la sierra dio bacantes
— ya que ninfas las niega ser errantes
    el hombro sin aljaba —;
    o — si del Termodonte 275
émulo el arroyuelo desatado

de aquel fragoso monte —
escuadrón de amazonas, desarmado,
tremola en sus riberas
280 pacíficas banderas.

Vulgo lascivo erraba
— al voto del mancebo,
el yugo de ambos sexos sacudido —
al tiempo que — de flores impedido
285 el que ya serenaba
la región de su frente rayo nuevo —
purpúrea terneruela, conducida
de su madre, no menos enramada,
entre albogues se ofrece, acompañada
290 de juventud florida.

Cuál dellos las pendientes sumas graves
de negras baja, de crestadas aves,
cuyo lascivo esposo vigilante
doméstico es del Sol nuncio canoro,
295 y — de coral barbado — no de oro
ciñe, sino de púrpura, turbante.

Quién la cerviz oprime
con la manchada copia
de los cabritos más retozadores,
300 tan golosos, que gime
el que menos peinar puede las flores
de su guirnalda propia.

No el sitio, no, fragoso,
no el torcido taladro de la tierra,
305 privilegió en la sierra
la paz del conejuelo temeroso;
trofeo ya su número es a un hombro,
si carga no y asombro.

Tú, ave peregrina,
310 arrogante esplendor — ya que no bello —
del último Occidente:

penda el rugoso nácar de tu frente
sobre el crespo zafiro de tu cuello,
que Himeneo a sus mesas te destina.

Sobre dos hombros larga vara ostenta 315
en cien aves cien picos de rubíes,
tafiletes calzadas carmesíes,
emulación y afrenta
aun de los berberiscos,
en la inculta región de aquellos riscos. 320

Lo que lloró la Aurora
— si es néctar lo que llora —,
y, antes que el Sol, enjuga
la abeja que madruga
a libar flores y a chupar cristales, 325
en celdas de oro líquido, en panales
la orza contenía
que un montañés traía.

No excedía la oreja
el pululante ramo 330
del ternezuelo gamo,
que mal llevar se deja,
y con razón: que el tálamo desdeña
la sombra aun de lisonja tan pequeña.

El arco del camino pues torcido, 335
— que habían con trabajo
por la fragosa cuerda del atajo
las gallardas serranas desmentido —
de la cansada juventud vencido,
— los fuertes hombros con las cargas graves, 340
treguas hechas süaves —
sueño le ofrece a quien buscó descanso
el ya sañudo arroyo, ahora manso:
merced de la hermosura que ha hospedado,
efectos, si no, dulces, del concento 345
que, en las lucientes de marfil clavijas,

las duras cuerdas de las negras guijas
hicieron a su curso acelerado,
en cuanto a su furor perdonó el viento.

350 Menos en renunciar tardó la encina
el extranjero errante,
que en reclinarse el menos fatigado
sobre la grana que se viste fina,
su bella amada, deponiendo amante
355 en las vestidas rosas su cuidado.

Saludólos a todos cortésmente,
y — admirado no menos
de los serranos que correspondido —
las sombras solicita de unas peñas.
360 De lágrimas los tiernos ojos llenos,
reconociendo el mar en el vestido
— que beberse no pudo el Sol ardiente
las que siempre dará cerúleas señas —,
político serrano,
365 de canas grave, habló desta manera:

'¿Cuál tigre, la más fiera
que clima infamó hircano,
dio el primer alimento
al que — ya deste o aquel mar — primero
370 surcó, labrador fiero,
el campo undoso en mal nacido pino,
vaga Clicie del viento,
en telas hecho — antes que en flor — el lino?
Más armas introdujo este marino
375 monstruo, escamado de robustas hayas,
a las que tanto mar divide playas,
que confusión y fuego
al frigio muro el otro leño griego.

Náutica industria investigó tal piedra,
380 que, cual abraza yedra
escollo, el metal ella fulminante
de que Marte se viste, y, lisonjera,

solicita el que más brilla diamante
en la nocturna capa de la esfera,
estrella a nuestro polo más vecina; 385
y, con virtud no poca,
distante la revoca,
elevada la inclina
ya de la Aurora bella
al rosado balcón, ya a la que sella 390
cerúlea tumba fría
las cenizas del día.

En esta, pues, fiándose, atractiva,
del Norte amante dura, alado roble,
no hay tormentoso cabo que no doble, 395
ni isla hoy a su vuelo fugitiva.
Tifis el primer leño mal seguro
condujo, muchos luego Palinuro;
si bien por un mar ambos, que la tierra
estanque dejó hecho, 400
cuyo famoso estrecho
una y otra de Alcides llave cierra.

Piloto hoy la Codicia, no de errantes
árboles, mas de selvas inconstantes,
al padre de las aguas Océano 405
— de cuya monarquía
el Sol, que cada día
nace en sus ondas y en sus ondas muere,
los términos saber todos no quiere —
dejó primero de su espuma cano, 410
sin admitir segundo
en inculcar sus límites al mundo.

Abetos suyos tres aquel tridente
violaron a Neptuno,
conculcado hasta allí de otro ninguno, 415
besando las que al Sol el Occidente
le corre en lecho azul de aguas marinas,
turquesadas cortinas.

A pesar luego de áspides volantes
420 — sombra del sol y tósigo del viento —
de caribes flechados, sus banderas
siempre gloriosas, siempre tremolantes,
rompieron los que armó de plumas ciento
lestrigones el istmo, aladas fieras:
425 el istmo que al Océano divide,
y — sierpe de cristal — juntar le impide
la cabeza, del Norte coronada,
con la que ilustra el Sur cola escamada
de antárticas estrellas.

430 Segundos leños dio a segundo polo
en nuevo mar, que le rindió no sólo
las blancas hijas de sus conchas bellas,
mas los que lograr bien no supo Midas
metales homicidas.

435 No le bastó después a este elemento
conducir orcas, alistar ballenas,
murarse de montañas espumosas,
infamar blanqueando sus arenas
con tantas del primer atrevimiento
440 señas — aun a los buitres lastimosas —,
para con estas lastimosas señas
temeridades enfrenar segundas.

Tú, Codicia, tú, pues, de las profundas
estigias aguas torpe marinero,
445 cuantos abre sepulcros el mar fiero
a tus huesos, desdeñas.

El promontorio que Éolo sus rocas
candados hizo de otras nuevas grutas
para el Austro de alas nunca enjutas,
450 para el Cierzo espirante por cien bocas,
doblaste alegre, y tu obstinada entena
cabo le hizo de Esperanza Buena.

Tantos luego astronómicos presagios
frustrados, tanta náutica doctrina,
debajo aun de la zona más vecina                455
al Sol, calmas vencidas y naufragios,
los reinos de la Aurora al fin besaste,
cuyos purpúreos senos perlas netas,
    cuyas minas secretas
hoy te guardan su más precioso engaste;                460
la aromática selva penetraste,
que al pájaro de Arabia — cuyo vuelo
    arco alado es del cielo,
    no corvo, mas tendido —
pira le erige, y le construye nido.                465

Zodíaco después fue cristalino
    a gloriöso pino,
émulo vago del ardiente coche
    del Sol, este elemento,
que cuatro veces había sido ciento                470
dosel al día y tálamo a la noche,
cuando halló de fugitiva plata
la bisagra, aunque estrecha, abrazadora
de un Océano y otro, siempre uno,
o las columnas bese o la escarlata,                475
    tapete de la aurora.
    Esta pues nave, ahora,
en el húmido templo de Neptuno
varada pende a la inmortal memoria
    con nombre de Victoria.                480

De firmes islas no la inmóvil flota
en aquel mar del Alba te describo,
cuyo número — ya que no lascivo —
por lo bello, agradable y por lo vario
la dulce confusión hacer podía,                485
que en los blancos estanques del Eurota
la virginal desnuda montería,

haciendo escollos o de mármol pario
o de terso marfil sus miembros bellos,
490 que pudo bien Acteón perderse en ellos.

El bosque dividido en islas pocas,
fragante productor de aquel aroma
— que, traducido mal por el Egito,
tarde le encomendó el Nilo a sus bocas,
495 y ellas más tarde a la gulosa Grecia —,
clavo no, espuela sí del apetito
— que cuanto en conocelle tardó Roma
fué templado Catón, casta Lucrecia —,
quédese, amigo, en tan inciertos mares,
500 donde con mi hacienda
del alma se quedó la mejor prenda,
cuya memoria es buitre de pesares.'

En suspiros con esto,
y en más anegó lágrimas el resto
505 de su discurso el montañés prolijo,
que el viento su caudal, el mar su hijo.

Consolallo pudiera el peregrino
con las de su edad corta historias largas,
si — vinculados todos a sus cargas,
510 cual próvidas hormigas a sus mieses —
no comenzaran ya los montañeses
a esconder con el número el camino,
y el cielo con el polvo. Enjugó el viejo
del tierno humor las venerables canas,
515 y levantando al forastero, dijo:

'Cabo me han hecho, hijo,
deste hermoso tercio de serranas;
si tu neutralidad sufre consejo,
y no te fuerza obligación precisa,
520 la piedad que en mi alma ya te hospeda
hoy te convida al que nos guarda sueño
política alameda,

verde muro de aquel lugar pequeño
que, a pesar de esos fresnos, se divisa;
sigue la femenil tropa conmigo: 525
verás curioso y honrarás testigo
el tálamo de nuestros labradores,
que de tu calidad señas mayores
me dan que del Océano tus paños,
o razón falta donde sobran años.' 530

Mal pudo el extranjero, agradecido,
en tercio tal negar tal compañía
y en tan noble ocasión tal hospedaje.
Alegres pisan la que, si no era
de chopos calle y de álamos carrera, 535
el fresco de los céfiros rüido,
el denso de los árboles celaje,
en duda ponen cuál mayor hacía
guerra al calor o resistencia al día.

Coros tejiendo, voces alternando, 540
sigue la dulce escuadra montañesa
del perezoso arroyo el paso lento,
    en cuanto él hurta blando,
entre los olmos que robustos besa,
pedazos de cristal, que el movimiento 545
libra en la falda, en el coturno ella,
    de la columna bella,
    ya que celosa basa,
dispensadora del cristal no escasa.

Sirenas de los montes su concento, 550
a la que menos del sañudo viento
    pudiera antigua planta
temer rüina o recelar fracaso,
pasos hiciera dar el menor paso
    de su pie o su garganta. 555

Pintadas aves — cítaras de pluma —
coronaban la bárbara capilla,
mientras el arroyuelo para oílla

hace de blanca espuma
560 tantas orejas cuantas guijas lava,
de donde es fuente adonde arroyo acaba.

Vencedores se arrogan los serranos
los consignados premios otro día,
ya al formidable salto, ya a la ardiente
565 lucha, ya a la carrera polvorosa.
El menos ágil, cuantos comarcanos
convoca el caso, él solo desafía,
consagrando los palios a su esposa,
que a mucha fresca rosa
570 beber el sudor hace de su frente,
mayor aún del que espera
en la lucha, en el salto, en la carrera.

Centro apacible un círculo espacioso
a más caminos que una estrella rayos,
575 hacía, bien de pobos, bien de alisos,
donde la Primavera,
— calzada abriles y vestida mayos —
centellas saca de cristal undoso
a un pedernal orlado de narcisos.
580 Este, pues, centro era
meta umbrosa al vaquero convecino,
y delicioso término al distante,
donde, aún cansado más que el caminante,
concurría el camino.

585 Al concento se abaten cristalino
sedientas las serranas,
cual simples codornices al reclamo
que les miente la voz, y verde cela,
entre la no espigada mies, la tela.
590 Músicas hojas viste el menor ramo
del álamo que peina verdes canas;
no céfiros en él, no ruiseñores
lisonjear pudieron breve rato

al montañés, que — ingrato
al fresco, a la armonía y a las flores — 595
del sitio pisa ameno
la fresca hierba, cual la arena ardiente
de la Libia, y a cuantas da la fuente
sierpes de aljófar, aún mayor veneno
que a las del Ponto, tímido, atribuye, 600
según el pie, según los labios huye.

Pasaron todos pues, y regulados
cual en los equinocios surcar vemos
los piélagos del aire libre algunas
volantes no galeras, 605
sino grullas veleras,
tal vez creciendo, tal menguando lunas
sus distantes extremos,
caracteres tal vez formando alados
en el papel diáfano del cielo 610
las plumas de su vuelo.

Ellas en tanto en bóvedas de sombras,
pintadas siempre al fresco,
cubren las que sidón telar turquesco
no ha sabido imitar verdes alfombras. 615

Apenas reclinaron la cabeza,
cuando, en número iguales y en belleza,
los márgenes matiza de las fuentes
segunda primavera de villanas,
que — parientas del novio aun más cercanas 620
que vecinos sus pueblos — de presentes
prevenidas, concurren a las bodas.

Mezcladas hacen todas
teatro dulce — no de escena muda —
el apacible sitio: espacio breve 625
en que, a pesar del sol, cuajada nieve,
y nieve de colores mil vestida,
la sombra vio florida
en la hierba menuda.

630 Viendo, pues, que igualmente les quedaba
para el lugar a ellas de camino
lo que al Sol para el lóbrego occidente,
cual de aves se caló turba canora
a robusto nogal que acequia lava
635 en cercado vecino,
cuando a nuestros antípodas la Aurora
las rosas gozar deja de su frente:
tal sale aquella que sin alas vuela
hermosa escuadra con ligero paso,
640 haciéndole atalayas del ocaso
cuantos humeros cuenta la aldehuela.

El lento escuadrón luego
alcanzan de serranos,
y — disolviendo allí la compañía —
645 al pueblo llegan con la luz que el día
cedió al sacro volcán de errante fuego,
a la torre, de luces coronada,
que el templo ilustra, y a los aires vanos
artificiosamente da exhalada
650 luminosas de pólvora saetas,
purpúreos no cometas.

Los fuegos, pues, el joven solemniza,
mientras el viejo tanta acusa tea
al de las bodas dios, no alguna sea
655 de nocturno Faetón carroza ardiente,
y miserablemente
campo amanezca estéril de ceniza
la que anocheció aldea.

De Alcides le llevó luego a las plantas,
660 que estaban, no muy lejos,
trenzándose el cabello verde a cuantas
da el fuego luces y el arroyo espejos.
Tanto garzón robusto,
tanta ofrecen los álamos zagala,

que abrevïara el Sol en una estrella, 665
por ver la menos bella,
cuantos saluda rayos el bengala,
del Ganges cisne adusto.

La gaita al baile solicita el gusto,
a la voz el salterio; 670
cruza el Trión más fijo el hemisferio,
y el tronco mayor danza en la ribera;
el eco, voz ya entera,
no hay silencio a que pronto no responda;
fanal es del arroyo cada onda, 675
luz el reflejo, la agua vidrïera.

Términos le da el sueño al regocijo,
mas al cansancio no: que el movimiento
verdugo de las fuerzas es prolijo.
Los fuegos — cuyas lenguas, ciento a ciento, 680
desmintieron la noche algunas horas,
cuyas luces, del sol competidoras,
fingieron día en la tiniebla oscura —
murieron, y en sí mismos sepultados,
sus miembros, en cenizas desatados, 685
piedras son de su misma sepultura.

Vence la noche al fin, y triunfa mudo
el silencio, aunque breve, del rüido:
sólo gime ofendido
el sagrado laurel del hierro agudo; 690
deja de su esplendor, deja desnudo
de su frondosa pompa al verde aliso
el golpe no remiso
del villano membrudo;
el que resistir pudo 695
al animoso Austro, al Euro ronco,
chopo gallardo — cuyo liso tronco
papel fue de pastores, aunque rudo —
a revelar secretos va a la aldea,
que impide Amor que aun otro chopo lea. 700

Estos árboles, pues, ve la mañana
mentir florestas, y emular viales
cuantos muró de líquidos cristales
    agricultura urbana.

705 Recordó al Sol, no, de su espuma cana,
la dulce de las aves armonía,
sino los dos topacios que batía
— orientales aldabas — Himeneo.
    Del carro, pues, febeo
710 el luminoso tiro,
mordiendo oro, el eclíptico zafiro
pisar quería, cuando el populoso
    lugarillo, el serrano
con su huésped, que admira cortesano
715 — a pesar del estambre y de la seda —
    el que tapiz frondoso
tejió de verdes hojas la arboleda,
y los que por las calles espaciosas
    fabrican arcos, rosas:
720 oblicuos nuevos pénsiles jardines,
de tantos como víolas jazmines.

Al galán novio el montañés presenta
su forastero; luego al venerable
padre de la que en sí bella se esconde
725 con ceño dulce, y, con silencio afable,
beldad parlera, gracia muda ostenta:
cual del rizado verde botón donde
abrevia su hermosura virgen rosa,
    las cisuras cairela
730 un color que la púrpura que cela
por brújula concede vergonzosa.
    Digna la juzga esposa
de un héroe, si no augusto, esclarecido,
el joven, al instante arrebatado
735 a la que, naufragante y desterrado,
    lo condenó a su olvido.

Este, pues, Sol que a olvido lo condena,
cenizas hizo las que su memoria
negras plumas vistió, que infelizmente
sordo engendran gusano, cuyo diente, 740
minador antes lento de su gloria,
inmortal arador fue de su pena.
Y en la sombra no más de la azucena,
que del clavel procura acompañada
imitar en la bella labradora 745
el templado color de la que adora,
víbora pisa tal el pensamiento,
que el alma, por los ojos desatada,
señas diera de su arrebatamiento,
si de zampoñas ciento 750
y de otros, aunque bárbaros, sonoros
instrumentos, no, en dos festivos coros,
vírgenes bellas, jóvenes lucidos,
llegaran conducidos.

El numeroso al fin de labradores 755
concurso impacïente
los novios saca: él, de años floreciente,
y de caudal más floreciente que ellos;
ella, la misma pompa de las flores,
la esfera misma de los rayos bellos. 760
El lazo de ambos cuellos
entre un lascivo enjambre iba de amores
Himeneo añudando,
mientras invocan su deidad la alterna
de zagalejas cándidas voz tierna 765
y de garzones este acento blando:

Coro I

Ven, Himeneo, ven donde te espera
con ojos y sin alas un Cupido,
cuyo cabello intonso dulcemente
niega el vello que el vulto ha colorido: 770
el vello, flores de su primavera,
y rayos el cabello de su frente.

Niño amó la que adora adolescente,
villana Psiques, ninfa labradora
775 de la tostada Ceres. Esta, ahora,
en los inciertos de su edad segunda
crepúsculos, vincule tu coyunda
a su ardiente deseo.
Ven, Himeneo, ven; ven, Himeneo.

Coro II

780 Ven, Himeneo, donde, entre arreboles
de honesto rosicler, previene el día
— aurora de sus ojos soberanos —
virgen tan bella, que hacer podría
tórrida la Noruega con dos soles,
785 y blanca la Etiopia con dos manos.
Claveles del abril, rubíes tempranos,
cuantos engasta el oro del cabello,
cuantas — del uno ya y del otro cuello
cadenas — la concordia engarza rosas,
790 de sus mejillas, siempre vergonzosas,
purpúreo son trofeo.
Ven, Himeneo, ven; ven, Himeneo.

Coro I

Ven, Himeneo, y plumas no vulgares
al aire los hijuelos den alados
795 de las que el bosque bellas ninfas cela;
de sus carcajes, éstos, argentados,
flechen mosquetas, nieven azahares;
vigilantes aquéllos, la aldehuela
rediman del que más o tardo vuela,
800 o infausto gime pájaro nocturno;
mudos coronen otros por su turno
el dulce lecho conjugal, en cuanto
lasciva abeja al virginal acanto
néctar le chupa hibleo.
805 Ven, Himeneo, ven; ven, Himeneo.

Coro II

Ven, Himeneo, y las volantes pías
que azules ojos con pestañas de oro
sus plumas son, conduzgan alta diosa,
gloria mayor del soberano coro.
Fíe tus nudos ella, que los días 810
disuelvan tarde en senectud dichosa;
y la que Juno es hoy a nuestra esposa,
casta Lucina — en lunas desiguales —
tantas veces repita sus umbrales,
que Níobe inmortal la admire el mundo, 815
no en blanco mármol, por su mal fecundo,
escollo hoy del Leteo.
Ven, Himeneo, ven; ven, Himeneo.

Coro I

Ven, Himeneo, y nuestra agricultura
de copia tal a estrellas deba amigas 820
progenie tan robusta, que su mano
toros dome, y de un rubio mar de espigas
inunde liberal la tierra dura;
y al verde, joven, floreciente llano
blancas ovejas suyas hagan, cano, 825
en breves horas caducar la hierba;
oro le expriman líquido a Minerva,
y — los olmos casando con las vides —
mientras coronan pámpanos a Alcides
clava empuñe Liëo. 830
Ven, Himeneo, ven; ven, Himeneo.

Coro II

Ven, Himeneo, y tantas le dé a Pales
cuantas a Palas dulces prendas esta
apenas hija hoy, madre mañana.
De errantes lilios unas la floresta 835
cubran: corderos mil, que los cristales
vistan del río en breve undosa lana;

de Aracnes otras la arrogancia vana
modestas acusando en blancas telas,
840 no los hurtos de amor, no las cautelas
de Júpiter compulsen: que, aun en lino,
ni a la pluvia luciente de oro fino,
ni al blanco cisne creo.
Ven, Himeneo, ven; ven, Himeneo.

845 El dulce alterno canto
a sus umbrales revocó felices
los novios, del vecino templo santo.
Del yugo aún no domadas las cervices,
novillos — breve término surcado —
850 restituyen así el pendiente arado
al que pajizo albergue los aguarda.

Llegaron todos pues, y, con gallarda
civil magnificencia, el suegro anciano,
cuantos la sierra dio, cuantos dio el llano
855 labradores convida
a la prolija rústica comida
que sin rumor previno en mesas grandes.

Ostente crespas blancas esculturas
artífice gentil de dobladuras
860 en los que damascó manteles Flandes,
mientras casero lino Ceres tanta
ofrece ahora, cuantos guardó el heno
dulces pomos, que al curso de Atalanta
fueran dorado freno.

865 Manjares que el veneno
y el apetito ignoran igualmente,
les sirvieron, y en oro, no, luciente,
confuso Baco, ni en bruñida plata
su néctar les desata,
870 sino en vidrio topacios carmesíes
y pálidos rubíes.

Sellar del fuego quiso regalado
los gulosos estómagos el rubio,
imitador süave de la cera,
quesillo — dulcemente apremïado  875
        de rústica, vaquera,
blanca, hermosa mano, cuyas venas
la distinguieron de la leche apenas —;
mas ni la encarcelada nuez esquiva,
ni el membrillo pudieran anudado,  880
        si la sabrosa oliva
no serenara el bacanal diluvio.

Levantadas las mesas, al canoro
son de la ninfa un tiempo, ahora caña,
seis de los montes, seis de la campaña,  885
— sus espaldas rayando el sutil oro
que negó al viento el nácar bien tejido —
terno de gracias bello, repetido
cuatro veces en doce labradoras,
entró bailando numerosamente;  890
y dulce musa entre ellas — si consiente
bárbaras el Parnaso moradoras —

        'Vivid felices,' dijo,
'largo curso de edad nunca prolijo;
y si prolijo, en nudos amorosos  895
        siempre vivid, esposos.
Venza no solo en su candor la nieve
mas plata en su esplendor sea cardada
cuanto estambre vital Cloto os traslada
de la alta fatal rueca al huso breve.  900

        Sean de la Fortuna
        aplausos la respuesta
        de vuestras granjerías.
        A la reja importuna,
        a la azada molesta  905
fecundo os rinda — en desiguales días —
        el campo agradecido
oro trillado y néctar exprimido.

Sus morados cantuesos, sus copadas
910 encinas la montaña contar antes
deje que vuestras cabras, siempre errantes,
que vuestras vacas, tarde o nunca herradas.

Corderillos os brote la ribera,
que la hierba menuda
915 y las perlas exceda del rocío
su número, y del río
la blanca espuma, cuantos la tijera
vellones les desnuda.

Tantos de breve fábrica, aunque ruda,
920 albergues vuestros las abejas moren,
y primaveras tantas os desfloren,
que — cual la Arabia madre ve de aromas
sacros troncos sudar fragantes gomas —
vuestros corchos por uno y otro poro
925 en dulce se desaten líquido oro.

Próspera, al fin, mas no espumosa tanto,
vuestra fortuna sea,
que alimenten la invidia en nuestra aldea
áspides más que en la región del llanto.
930 Entre opulencias y necesidades,
medianías vinculen competentes
a vuestros descendientes
— previniendo ambos daños — las edades.
Ilustren obeliscos las ciudades,
935 a los rayos de Júpiter expuesta
— aún más que a los de Febo — su corona,
cuando a la choza pastoral perdona
el cielo, fulminando la floresta.

Cisnes pues una y otra pluma, en esta
940 tranquilidad os halle labradora
la postrimera hora:
cuya lámina cifre desengaños,
que en letras pocas lean muchos años.'

Del himno culto dio el último acento
fin mudo al baile, al tiempo que seguida 945
la novia sale de villanas ciento
a la verde florida palizada,
cual nueva fénix en flamantes plumas
matutinos del sol rayos vestida,
de cuanta surca el aire acompañada 950
monarquía canora;
y, vadeando nubes, las espumas
del rey corona de los otros ríos:
en cuya orilla el viento hereda ahora
pequeños no vacíos 955
de funerales bárbaros trofeos
que el Egipto erigió a sus Ptolomeos.

Los árboles que el bosque habían fingido,
umbroso coliseo ya formando,
despejan el ejido, 960
olímpica palestra
de valientes desnudos labradores.

Llegó la desposada apenas, cuando
feroz ardiente muestra
hicieron dos robustos luchadores 965
de sus músculos, menos defendidos
del blanco lino que del vello obscuro.
Abrazáronse, pues, los dos, y luego
— humo anhelando el que no suda fuego —
de recíprocos nudos impedidos 970
cual duros olmos de implicantes vides,
yedra el uno es tenaz del otro muro.
Mañosos, al fin, hijos de la tierra,
cuando fuertes no Alcides,
procuran derribarse, y, derribados, 975
cual pinos se levantan arraigados
en los profundos senos de la sierra.
Premio los honra igual. Y de otros cuatro
ciñe las sienes gloriosa rama,
con que se puso término a la lucha. 980

Las dos partes rayaba del teatro
el sol, cuando arrogante joven llama
al expedido salto
la bárbara corona que le escucha.
985 Arras del animoso desafío
un pardo gabán fue en el verde suelo,
a quien se abaten ocho o diez soberbios
montañeses, cual suele de lo alto
calarse turba de invidiosas aves
990 a los ojos de Ascálafo, vestido
de perezosas plumas. Quién, de graves
piedras las duras manos impedido,
su agilidad pondera; quién sus nervios
desata estremeciéndose gallardo.
995 Besó la raya pues el pie desnudo
del suelto mozo, y con airoso vuelo
pisó del viento lo que del ejido
tres veces ocupar pudiera un dardo.

La admiración, vestida un mármol frío,
1000 apenas arquear las cejas pudo;
la emulación, calzada un duro hielo,
torpe se arraiga. Bien que impulso noble
de gloria, aunque villano, solicita
a un vaquero de aquellos montes, grueso,
1005 membrudo, fuerte roble,
que, ágil a pesar de lo robusto,
al aire se arrebata, violentando
lo grave tanto, que lo precipita
— Ícaro montañés — su mismo peso,
1010 de la menuda hierba el seno blando
piélago duro hecho a su rüina.

Si no tan corpulento, más adusto
serrano le sucede,
que iguala y aun excede
1015 al ayuno leopardo,

al corcillo travieso, al muflón sardo
que de las rocas trepa a la marina
    sin dejar ni aun pequeña
del pie ligero bipartida seña.
Con más felicidad que el precedente, 1020
pisó las huellas casi del primero
    el adusto vaquero.
Pasos otro dio al aire, al suelo coces.

Y premïados graduadamente,
advocaron a sí toda la gente 1025
— cierzos del llano y austros de la sierra —
    mancebos tan veloces,
que cuando Ceres más dora la tierra,
y argenta el mar desde sus grutas hondas
    Neptuno, sin fatiga 1030
    su vago pie de pluma
surcar pudiera mieses, pisar ondas,
    sin inclinar espiga,
    sin vïolar espuma.

Dos veces eran diez, y dirigidos 1035
a dos olmos que quieren, abrazados,
ser palios verdes, ser frondosas metas,
    salen cual de torcidos
arcos, o nervïosos o acerados,
con silbo igual, dos veces diez saetas. 1040

    No el polvo desparece
el campo, que no pisan alas hierba;
es el más torpe una herida cierva,
el más tardo la vista desvanece,
y, siguiendo al más lento, 1045
    cojea el pensamiento.

El tercio casi de una milla era
    la prolija carrera
que los hercúleos troncos hace breves;

1050 pero las plantas leves
de tres sueltos zagales
la distancia sincopan tan iguales,
que la atención confunden judiciosa.

De la Peneida virgen desdeñosa,
1055 los dulces fugitivos miembros bellos
en la corteza no abrazó, reciente,
más firme Apolo, más estrechamente,
que de una y otra meta gloriosa
las duras basas abrazaron ellos
1060 con triplicado nudo.
Árbitro Alcides en sus ramas, dudo
que el caso decidiera,
bien que su menor hoja un ojo fuera
del lince más agudo.

1065 En tanto pues que el palio neutro pende
y la carroza de la luz desciende
a templarse en las ondas, Himeneo
— por templar, en los brazos, el deseo
del galán novio, de la esposa bella —
1070 los rayos anticipa de la estrella,
cerúlea ahora, ya purpúrea guía
de los dudosos términos del día.

El jüicio — al de todos, indeciso —
del concurso ligero,
1075 el padrino con tres de limpio acero
cuchillos corvos absolvello quiso.
Solícita Junón, Amor no omiso,
al son de otra zampoña que conduce
ninfas bellas y sátiros lascivos,
1080 los desposados a su casa vuelven,
que coronada luce
de estrellas fijas, de astros fugitivos
que en sonoroso humo se resuelven.

Llegó todo el lugar, y, despedido,
casta Venus — que el lecho ha prevenido 1085
de las plumas que baten más süaves
en su volante carro blancas aves —
los novios entra en dura no estacada:
que, siendo Amor una deidad alada,
bien previno la hija de la espuma 1090
a batallas de amor campo de pluma.

## II 'FÁBULA DE POLIFEMO Y GALATEA'

(1613)

Estas que me dictó rimas sonoras,
culta sí, aunque bucólica, Talía
— ¡oh excelso conde! — , en las purpúreas horas
que es rosas la alba y rosicler el día,
5 ahora que de luz tu Niebla doras,
escucha, al son de la zampoña mía,
si ya los muros no te ven, de Huelva,
peinar el viento, fatigar la selva.

Templado, pula en la maestra mano
10 el generoso pájaro su pluma,
o tan mudo en la alcándara, que en vano
aun desmentir al cascabel presuma;
tascando haga el freno de oro, cano,
del caballo andaluz la ociosa espuma;
15 gima el lebrel en el cordón de seda.
Y al cuerno, al fin, la cítara suceda.

Treguas al ejercicio sean robusto,
ocio atento, silencio dulce, en cuanto
debajo escuchas de dosel augusto,
20 del músico jayán el fiero canto.
Alterna con las Musas hoy el gusto;
que si la mía puede ofrecer tanto
clarín (y de la Fama no segundo),
tu nombre oirán los términos del mundo.

25 Donde espumoso el mar sicilïano
el pie argenta de plata al Lilibeo
(bóveda o de las fraguas de Vulcano,
o tumba de los huesos de Tifeo),
pálidas señas cenizoso un llano
30 — cuando no del sacrílego deseo —
del duro oficio da. Allí una alta roca
mordaza es a una gruta, de su boca.

Guarnición tosca de este escollo duro
troncos robustos son, a cuya greña
menos luz debe, menos aire puro 35
la caverna profunda, que a la peña;
caliginoso lecho, el seno obscuro
ser de la negra noche nos lo enseña
infame turba de nocturnas aves,
gimiendo tristes y volando graves. 40

De este, pues, formidable de la tierra
bostezo, el melancólico vacío
a Polifemo, horror de aquella sierra,
bárbara choza es, albergue umbrío
y redil espacioso donde encierra 45
cuanto las cumbres ásperas cabrío,
de los montes, esconde: copia bella
que un silbo junta y un peñasco sella.

Un monte era de miembros eminente
este (que, de Neptuno hijo fiero, 50
de un ojo ilustra el orbe de su frente,
émulo casi del mayor lucero)
cíclope, a quien el pino más valiente,
bastón, le obedecía, tan ligero,
y al grave peso junco tan delgado, 55
que un día era bastón y otro cayado.

Negro el cabello, imitador undoso
de las obscuras aguas del Leteo,
al viento que lo peina proceloso,
vuela sin orden, pende sin aseo; 60
un torrente es su barba impetüoso,
que (adusto hijo de este Pirineo)
su pecho inunda, o tarde, o mal, o en vano
surcada aun de los dedos de su mano.

No la Trinacria en sus montañas, fiera 65
armó de crüeldad, calzó de viento,
que redima feroz, salve ligera,

su piel manchada de colores ciento:
pellico es ya la que en los bosques era
70 mortal horror al que con paso lento
los bueyes a su albergue reducía,
pisando la dudosa luz del día.

Cercado es (cuanto más capaz, más lleno)
de la fruta, el zurrón, casi abortada,
75 que el tardo otoño deja al blando seno
de la piadosa hierba, encomendada:
la serba, a quien le da rugas el heno;
la pera, de quien fue cuna dorada
la rubia paja, y — pálida tutora —
80 la niega avara, y pródiga la dora.

Erizo es el zurrón, de la castaña,
y (entre el membrillo o verde o datilado)
de la manzana hipócrita, que engaña,
a lo pálido no, a lo arrebolado,
85 y, de la encina (honor de la montaña,
que pabellón al siglo fue dorado)
el tributo, alimento, aunque grosero,
del mejor mundo, del candor primero.

Cera y cáñamo unió (que no debiera)
90 cien cañas, cuyo bárbaro rüído,
de más ecos que unió cáñamo y cera
albogues, duramente es repetido.
La selva se confunde, el mar se altera,
rompe Tritón su caracol torcido,
95 sordo huye el bajel a vela y remo:
¡tal la música es de Polifemo!

Ninfa, de Doris hija, la más bella,
adora, que vio el reino de la espuma.
Galatea es su nombre, y dulce en ella
100 el terno Venus de sus Gracias suma.

Son una y otra luminosa estrella
lucientes ojos de su blanca pluma:
si roca de cristal no es de Neptuno,
pavón de Venus es, cisne de Juno.

Purpúreas rosas sobre Galatea 105
la Alba entre lilios cándidos deshoja:
duda el Amor cuál más su color sea,
o púrpura nevada, o nieve roja.
De su frente la perla es, eritrea,
émula vana. El ciego dios se enoja, 110
y, condenado su esplendor, la deja
pender en oro al nácar de su oreja.

Invidia de las ninfas y cuidado
de cuantas honra el mar deidades era;
pompa del marinero niño alado 115
que sin fanal conduce su venera.
Verde el cabello, el pecho no escamado,
ronco sí, escucha a Glauco la ribera
inducir a pisar la bella ingrata,
en carro de cristal, campos de plata. 120

Marino joven, las cerúleas sienes,
del más tierno coral ciñe Palemo,
rico de cuantos la agua engendra bienes,
del Faro odioso al promontorio extremo;
mas en la gracia igual, si en los desdenes 125
perdonado algo más que Polifemo,
de la que, aún no le oyó, y, calzada plumas,
tantas flores pisó como él espumas.

Huye la ninfa bella; y el marino
amante nadador, ser bien quisiera, 130
ya que no áspid a su pie divino,
dorado pomo a su veloz carrera;
mas, ¿cuál diente mortal, cuál metal fino
la fuga suspender podrá ligera
que el desdén solicita? ¡Oh cuánto yerra 135
delfín que sigue en agua corza en tierra!

Sicilia, en cuanto oculta, en cuanto ofrece,
copa es de Baco, huerto de Pomona:
tanto de frutas ésta la enriquece,
140 cuanto aquél de racimos la corona.
En carro que estival trillo parece,
a sus campañas Ceres no perdona,
de cuyas siempre fértiles espigas
las provincias de Europa son hormigas.

145 A Pales su viciosa cumbre debe
lo que a Ceres, y aún más, su vega llana;
pues si en la una granos de oro llueve,
copos nieva en la otra mil de lana.
De cuantos siegan oro, esquilan nieve,
150 o en pipas guardan la exprimida grana,
bien sea religión, bien amor sea,
deidad, aunque sin templo, es Galatea.

Sin aras, no: que el margen donde para
del espumoso mar su pie ligero,
155 al labrador, de sus primicias ara,
de sus esquilmos es al ganadero;
de la Copia a la tierra poco avara
el cuerno vierte el hortelano, entero,
sobre la mimbre que tejió, prolija,
160 si artificiosa no, su honesta hija.

Arde la juventud, y los arados
peinan las tierras que surcaron antes,
mal conducidos, cuando no arrastrados
de tardos bueyes, cual su dueño errantes;
165 sin pastor que los silbe, los ganados
los crujidos ignoran resonantes
de las hondas, si, en vez del pastor pobre,
el céfiro no silba, o cruje el robre.

Mudo la noche el can, el día, dormido,
170 de cerro en cerro y sombra en sombra yace.
Bala el ganado; al mísero balido,
nocturno el lobo de las sombras nace.

Cébase; y fiero, deja humedecido
en sangre de una lo que la otra pace.
¡Revoca, Amor, los silbos, o a su dueño 175
el silencio del can siga, y el sueño!

La fugitiva ninfa, en tanto, donde
hurta un laurel su tronco al sol ardiente,
tantos jazmines cuanta hierba esconde
la nieve de sus miembros, da a una fuente. 180
Dulce se queja, dulce le responde
un ruiseñor a otro, y dulcemente
al sueño da sus ojos la armonía,
por no abrasar con tres soles el día.

Salamandria del Sol, vestido estrellas, 185
latiendo el Can del cielo estaba, cuando
(polvo el cabello, húmidas centellas,
si no ardientes aljófares, sudando)
llegó Acis; y, de ambas luces bellas
dulce Occidente viendo al sueño blando, 190
su boca dio, y sus ojos cuanto pudo,
al sonoro cristal, al cristal mudo.

Era Acis un venablo de Cupido,
de un fauno, medio hombre, medio fiera,
en Simetis, hermosa ninfa, habido; 195
gloria del mar, honor de su ribera.
El bello imán, el ídolo dormido,
que acero sigue, idólatra venera,
rico de cuanto el huerto ofrece pobre,
rinden las vacas y fomenta el robre. 200

El celestial humor recién cuajado
que la almendra guardó entre verde y seca,
en blanca mimbre se lo puso al lado,
y un copo, en verdes juncos, de manteca;
en breve corcho, pero bien labrado, 205
un rubio hijo de una encina hueca,
dulcísimo panal, a cuya cera
su néctar vinculó la primavera.

Caluroso, al arroyo da las manos,
210 y con ellas las ondas a su frente,
entre dos mirtos que, de espuma canos,
dos verdes garzas son de la corriente.
Vagas cortinas de volantes vanos
corrió Favonio lisonjeramente
215 a la (de viento cuando no sea) cama
de frescas sombras, de menuda grama.

La ninfa, pues, la sonorosa plata
bullir sintió del arroyuelo apenas,
cuando, a los verdes márgenes ingrata,
220 segur se hizo de sus azucenas.
Huyera; mas tan frío se desata
un temor perezoso por sus venas,
que a la precisa fuga, al presto vuelo,
grillos de nieve fue, plumas de hielo.

225 Fruta en mimbres halló, leche exprimida
en juncos, miel en corcho, mas sin dueño;
si bien al dueño debe, agradecida,
su deidad culta, venerado el sueño.
A la ausencia mil veces ofrecida,
230 este de cortesía no pequeño
indicio la dejó — aunque estatua helada —
más discursiva y menos alterada.

No al Cíclope atribuye, no, la ofrenda;
no a sátiro lascivo, ni a otro feo
235 morador de las selvas, cuya rienda
el sueño aflija, que aflojó el deseo.
El niño dios, entonces, de la venda,
ostentación gloriosa, alto trofeo
quiere que al árbol de su madre sea
240 el desdén hasta allí de Galatea.

Entre las ramas del que más se lava
en el arroyo, mirto levantado,
carcaj de cristal hizo, si no aljaba,
su blanco pecho, de un arpón dorado.

El monstro de rigor, la fiera brava, 245
mira la ofrenda ya con más cuidado,
y aun siente que a su dueño sea, devoto,
confuso alcaide más, el verde soto.

Llamáralo, aunque muda, mas no sabe
el nombre articular que más querría; 250
ni lo ha visto, si bien pincel süave
lo ha bosquejado ya en su fantasía.
Al pie — no tanto ya, del temor, grave —
fía su intento; y, tímida, en la umbría
cama de campo y campo de batalla, 255
fingiendo sueño al cauto garzón halla.

El bulto vio, y, haciéndolo dormido,
librada en un pie toda sobre él pende
(urbana al sueño, bárbara al mentido
retórico silencio que no entiende): 260
no el ave reina, así, el fragoso nido
corona inmóvil, mientras no desciende
— rayo con plumas — al milano pollo
que la eminencia abriga de un escollo,

como la ninfa bella, compitiendo 265
con el garzón dormido en cortesía,
no sólo para, mas el dulce estruendo
del lento arroyo enmudecer querría.
A pesar luego de las ramas, viendo
colorido el bosquejo que ya había 270
en su imaginación Cupido hecho
con el pincel que le clavó su pecho,

de sitio mejorada, atenta mira,
en la disposición robusta, aquello
que, si por lo süave no la admira, 275
es fuerza que la admire por lo bello.
Del casi tramontado sol aspira
a los confusos rayos, su cabello;
flores su bozo es, cuyas colores,
como duerme la luz, niegan las flores. 280

En la rústica greña yace oculto
el áspid, del intonso prado ameno,
antes que del peinado jardín culto
en el lascivo, regalado seno:
285 en lo viril desata de su vulto
lo más dulce el Amor, de su veneno;
bébelo Galatea, y da otro paso
por apurarle la ponzoña al vaso.

Acis — aún más de aquello que dispensa
290 la brújula del sueño vigilante —,
alterada la ninfa esté o suspensa,
Argos es siempre atento a su semblante,
lince penetrador de lo que piensa,
cíñalo bronce o múrelo diamante:
295 que en sus paladïones Amor ciego,
sin romper muros, introduce fuego.

El sueño de sus miembros sacudido,
gallardo el joven la persona ostenta,
y al marfil luego de sus pies rendido,
300 el coturno besar dorado intenta.
Menos ofende el rayo prevenido,
al marinero, menos la tormenta
prevista le turbó o pronosticada:
Galatea lo diga, salteada.

305 Más agradable y menos zahareña,
al mancebo levanta venturoso,
dulce ya concediéndole y risueña,
paces no al sueño, treguas sí al reposo.
Lo cóncavo hacía de una peña
310 a un fresco sitïal dosel umbroso,
y verdes celosías unas hiedras,
trepando troncos y abrazando piedras.

Sobre una alfombra, que imitara en vano
el tirio sus matices (si bien era
315 de cuantas sedas ya hiló, gusano,

y, artífice, tejió la Primavera)
reclinados, al mirto más lozano,
una y otra lasciva, si ligera,
paloma se caló, cuyos gemidos
— trompas de amor — alteran sus oídos. 320

El ronco arrullo al joven solicita;
mas, con desvíos Galatea suaves,
a su audacia los términos limita,
y el aplauso al concento de las aves.
Entre las ondas y la fruta, imita 325
Acis al siempre ayuno en penas graves:
que, en tanta gloria, infierno son no breve,
fugitivo cristal, pomos de nieve.

No a las palomas concedió Cupido
juntar de sus dos picos los rubíes, 330
cuando al clavel el joven atrevido
las dos hojas le chupa carmesíes.
Cuantas produce Pafo, engendra Gnido,
negras vïolas, blancos alhelíes,
llueven sobre el que Amor quiere que sea 335
tálamo de Acis ya y de Galatea.

Su aliento humo, sus relinchos fuego,
si bien su freno espumas, ilustraba
las columnas Etón que erigió el griego,
do el carro de la luz sus ruedas lava, 340
cuando, de amor el fiero jayán ciego,
la cerviz oprimió a una roca brava,
que a la playa, de escollos no desnuda,
linterna es ciega y atalaya muda.

Árbitro de montañas y ribera, 345
aliento dio, en la cumbre de la roca,
a los albogues que agregó la cera,
el prodigioso fuelle de su boca;
la ninfa los oyó, y ser más quisiera

350 breve flor, hierba humilde, tierra poca,
que de su nuevo tronco vid lasciva,
muerta de amor, y de temor no viva.

Mas — cristalinos pámpanos sus brazos —
amor la implica, si el temor la anuda,
355 al infelice olmo que pedazos
la segur de los celos hará aguda.
Las cavernas en tanto, los ribazos
que ha prevenido la zampoña ruda,
el trueno de la voz fulminó luego:
360 ¡referidlo, Pïérides, os ruego!

'¡Oh bella Galatea, más süave
que los claveles que tronchó la aurora;
blanca más que las plumas de aquel ave
que dulce muere y en las aguas mora;
365 igual en pompa al pájaro que, grave,
su manto azul de tantos ojos dora
cuantas el celestial zafiro estrellas!
¡Oh tú, que en dos incluyes las más bellas!

'Deja las ondas, deja el rubio coro
370 de las hijas de Tetis, y el mar vea,
cuando niega la luz un carro de oro,
que en dos la restituye Galatea.
Pisa la arena, que en la arena adoro
cuantas el blanco pie conchas platea,
375 cuyo bello contacto puede hacerlas,
sin concebir rocío, parir perlas.

'Sorda hija del mar, cuyas orejas
a mis gemidos son rocas al viento:
o dormida te hurten a mis quejas
380 purpúreos troncos de corales ciento,
o al disonante número de almejas
— marino, si agradable no, instrumento —
coros tejiendo estés, escucha un día
mi voz, por dulce, cuando no por mía.

'Pastor soy, mas tan rico de ganados, 385
que los valles impido más vacíos,
los cerros desparezco levantados
y los caudales seco de los ríos;
no los que, de sus ubres desatados,
o derivados de los ojos míos, 390
leche corren y lágrimas; que iguales
en número a mis bienes son mis males.

'Sudando néctar, lambicando olores,
senos que ignora aun la golosa cabra,
corchos me guardan, más que abeja flores 395
liba inquïeta, ingenïosa labra;
troncos me ofrecen árboles mayores,
cuyos enjambres, o el abril los abra,
o los desate el mayo, ámbar distilan
y en ruecas de oro rayos del sol hilan. 400

'Del Júpiter soy hijo, de las ondas,
aunque pastor; si tu desdén no espera
a que el monarca de esas grutas hondas,
en trono de cristal te abrace nuera,
Polifemo te llama, no te escondas; 405
que tanto esposo admira la ribera
cual otro no vio Febo, más robusto,
del perezoso Volga al Indo adusto.

'Sentado, a la alta palma no perdona
su dulce fruto mi robusta mano; 410
en pie, sombra capaz es mi persona
de innumerables cabras el verano.
¿Qué mucho, si de nubes se corona
por igualarme la montaña en vano,
y en los cielos, desde esta roca, puedo 415
escribir mis desdichas con el dedo?

'Marítimo alcïón roca eminente
sobre sus huevos coronaba, el día
que espejo de zafiro fue luciente
la playa azul, de la persona mía. 420

Miréme, y lucir vi un sol en mi frente,
cuando en el cielo un ojo se veía:
neutra el agua dudaba a cuál fe preste,
o al cielo humano, o al cíclope celeste.

425 'Registra en otras puertas el venado
sus años, su cabeza colmilluda
la fiera cuyo cerro levantado,
de helvecias picas es muralla aguda;
la humana suya el caminante errado
430 dio ya a mi cueva, de piedad desnuda,
albergue hoy, por tu causa, al peregrino,
do halló reparo, si perdió camino.

'En tablas dividida, rica nave
besó la playa miserablemente,
435 de cuantas vomitó riquezas grave,
por las bocas del Nilo el Orïente.
Yugo aquel día, y yugo bien süave,
del fiero mar a la sañuda frente
imponiéndole estaba (si no al viento
440 dulcísimas coyundas) mi instrumento,

'cuando, entre globos de agua, entregar veo
a las arenas ligurina haya,
en cajas los aromas del Sabeo,
en cofres las riquezas de Cambaya:
445 delicias de aquel mundo, ya trofeo
de Escila, que, ostentado en nuestra playa,
lastimoso despojo fue dos días
a las que esta montaña engendra arpías.

'Segunda tabla a un ginovés mi gruta
450 de su persona fue, de su hacienda;
la una reparada, la otra enjuta,
relación del naufragio hizo horrenda.
Luciente paga de la mejor fruta
que en hierbas se recline, en hilos penda,
455 colmillo fue del animal que el Ganges
sufrir muros le vio, romper falanges:

'arco, digo, gentil, bruñida aljaba,
obras ambas de artífice prolijo,
y de Malaco rey a deidad Java
alto don, según ya mi huésped dijo. 460
De aquél la mano, de ésta el hombro agrava;
convencida la madre, imita al hijo:
serás a un tiempo en estos horizontes
Venus del mar, Cupido de los montes.'

Su horrenda voz, no su dolor interno, 465
cabras aquí le interrumpieron, cuantas
— vagas el pie, sacrílegas el cuerno —
a Baco se atrevieron en sus plantas.
Mas, conculcado el pámpano más tierno
viendo el fiero pastor, voces él tantas, 470
y tantas despidió la honda piedras,
que el muro penetraron de las hiedras.

De los nudos, con esto, más süaves,
los dulces dos amantes desatados,
por duras guijas, por espinas graves 475
solicitan el mar con pies alados:
tal, redimiendo de importunas aves
incauto meseguero sus sembrados,
de liebres dirimió copia, así, amiga,
que vario sexo unió y un surco abriga. 480

Viendo el fiero jayán, con paso mudo
correr al mar la fugitiva nieve
(que a tanta vista el líbico desnudo
registra el campo de su adarga breve)
y al garzón viendo, cuantas mover pudo 485
celoso trueno, antiguas hayas mueve:
tal, antes que la opaca nube rompa,
previene rayo fulminante trompa.

Con vïolencia desgajó infinita,
la mayor punta de la excelsa roca, 490
que al joven, sobre quien la precipita,
urna es mucha, pirámide no poca.

Con lágrimas la ninfa solicita
las deidades del mar, que Acis invoca:
495 concurren todas, y el peñasco duro
la sangre que exprimió, cristal fue puro.

Sus miembros lastimosamente opresos
del escollo fatal fueron apenas,
que los pies de los árboles más gruesos
500 calzó el líquido aljófar de sus venas.
Corriente plata al fin sus blancos huesos,
lamiendo flores y argentando arenas,
a Doris llega, que, con llanto pío,
yerno lo saludó, lo aclamó río.

## III SONNETS

### I

(1582)

¡Oh claro honor del líquido elemento,
dulce arroyuelo de corriente plata
cuya agua entre la yerba se dilata
con regalado son, con paso lento!
Pues la por quien helar y arder me siento, 5
mientras en ti se mira, Amor retrata
de su rostro la nieve y la escarlata
en tu tranquilo y blando movimiento,
vête como te vas; no dejes floja
la undosa rienda al cristalino freno 10
con que gobiernas tu veloz corriente;
que no es bien que confusamente acoja
tanta belleza en su profundo seno
el gran señor del húmido tridente.

### 2

(1582)

Mientras por competir con tu cabello
oro bruñido al sol relumbra en vano,
mientras con menosprecio en medio el llano
mira tu blanca frente el lilio bello;
mientras a cada labio, por cogello, 5
siguen más ojos que al clavel temprano,
y mientras triunfa con desdén lozano,
del luciente cristal tu gentil cuello;
goza cuello, cabello, labio y frente,
antes que lo que fue en tu edad dorada 10
oro, lilio, clavel, cristal luciente,
no sólo en plata o vïola troncada
se vuelva, mas tú y ello juntamente
en tierra, en humo, en polvo, en sombra, en nada.

## 3

(1584)

La dulce boca que a gustar convida
un humor entre perlas distilado
y a no invidiar aquel licor sagrado
que a Júpiter ministra el garzón de Ida,
amantes, no toquéis, si queréis vida;
porque entre un labio y otro colorado
Amor está, de su veneno armado,
cual entre flor y flor sierpe escondida.
No os engañen las rosas que a la Aurora
diréis que aljofaradas y olorosas
se le cayeron del purpúreo seno;
manzanas son de Tántalo, y no rosas,
que después huyen del que incitan hora
y sólo del Amor queda el veneno.

## 4

(1585)

*A Córdoba*

¡Oh excelso muro, oh torres coronadas
de honor, de majestad, de gallardía!
¡Oh gran río, gran rey de Andalucía,
de arenas nobles, ya que no doradas!
¡Oh fértil llano, oh sierras levantadas,
que privilegia el cielo y dora el día!
¡Oh siempre gloriosa patria mía,
tanto por plumas cuanto por espadas!
¡Si entre aquellas ruinas y despojos
que enriquece Genil y Dauro baña
tu memoria no fue alimento mío,
nunca merezcan mis ausentes ojos
ver tu muro, tus torres y tu río,
tu llano y sierra, oh patria, oh flor de España!

## 5

(1594)

*De un caminante enfermo que se enamoró donde fue hospedado*

Descaminado, enfermo, peregrino,
en tenebrosa noche, con pie incierto,
la confusión pisando del desierto,
voces en vano dio, pasos sin tino.
Repetido latir, si no vecino, 5
distincto oyó de can siempre despierto,
y en pastoral albergue mal cubierto
piedad halló, si no halló camino.
Salió el Sol, y entre armiños escondida,
soñolienta beldad con dulce saña 10
salteó al no bien sano pasajero.
Pagará el hospedaje con la vida;
más le valiera errar en la montaña
que morir de la suerte que yo muero.

## 6

(1611)

*Del túmulo que hizo Córdoba en las honras de la señora reina doña Margarita*

Máquina funeral, que desta vida
nos decís la mudanza estando queda,
pira, no de aromática arboleda,
sí a más gloriosa fénix construída;
bajel en cuya gavia esclarecida 5
estrellas, hijas de otra mejor Leda,
serenan la Fortuna, de su rueda
la volubilidad reconocida,
farol luciente sois, que solicita
la razón, entre escollos naufragante 10
al puerto; y a pesar de lo luciente,
oscura concha de una Margarita,
que, rubí en caridad, en fe diamante,
renace en nuevo Sol, en nuevo Oriente.

## 7

(1614)

*Inscripción para el sepulcro de Domínico Greco*

Esta en forma elegante, oh peregrino,
de pórfido luciente dura llave,
el pincel niega al mundo más süave,
que dio espíritu a leño, vida a lino.
5 Su nombre, aún de mayor aliento dino
que en los clarines de la Fama cabe,
el campo ilustra de ese mármol grave:
venéralo y prosigue tu camino.
Yace el Griego. Heredó Naturaleza
10 Arte; y el Arte, estudio. Iris, colores.
Febo, luces — si no sombras, Morfeo —.
Tanta urna, a pesar de su dureza,
lágrimas beba, y cuantos suda olores
corteza funeral de árbol sabeo.

## 8

(1623)

*Infiere, de los achaques de la vejez, cercano el fin a que católico se alienta*

En este occidental, en este, oh Licio,
climatérico lustro de tu vida,
todo mal afirmado pie es caída,
toda fácil caída es precipicio.
5 ¿Caduca el paso? Ilústrese el juicio.
Desatándose va la tierra unida.
¿Qué prudencia, del polvo prevenida,
la rüina aguardó del edificio?
La piel, no sólo sierpe venenosa,
10 mas con la piel los años se desnuda,
y el hombre no. ¡Ciego discurso humano!
¡Oh aquel dichoso, que, la ponderosa
porción depuesta en una piedra muda,
la leve da al zafiro soberano!

## 9

(1623)

*De la brevedad engañosa de la vida*

Menos solicitó veloz saeta
destinada señal, que mordió aguda;
agonal carro por la arena muda
no coronó con más silencio meta,
que presurosa corre, que secreta 5
a su fin nuestra edad. A quien lo duda,
fiera que sea de razón desnuda,
cada sol repetido es un cometa.
¿Confiésalo Cartago, y tú lo ignoras?
Peligro corres, Licio, si porfías 10
en seguir sombras y abrazar engaños.
Mal te perdonarán a ti las horas;
las horas que limando están los días,
los días que royendo están los años.

## 10

(1623)

*Al Conde-duque de Olivares*

En la capilla estoy y condenado
a partir sin remedio de esta vida;
siento la causa aun más que la partida,
por hambre expulso como sitïado.
Culpa sin duda es ser desdichado, 5
mayor de condición ser encogida;
de ellas me acuso en esta despedida,
y partiré a lo menos confesado.
Examine mi suerte el hierro agudo,
que a pesar de sus filos me prometo 10
alto piedad de vuestra excelsa mano.
Ya que el encogimiento ha sido mudo,
los números, Señor, de este soneto
lenguas sean y lágrimas no en vano.

## II

(1623)

*Determinado a dejar sus pretensiones y volverse a Córdoba*

De la merced, señores, despedido,
pues lo ha querido así la suerte mía,
de mis deudos iré a la compañía,
no poco de mis deudas oprimido.
5 Si haber sido del Carmen culpa ha sido,
sobra el que se me dio hábito un día:
huélgome que es templada Andalucía,
ya que vuelvo descalzo al patrio nido.
Mínimo, pues, si capellán indino
10 del mayor Rey, monarca al fin de cuanto
pisa el Sol, lamen ambos océanos,
la fuerza obedeciendo del destino,
el cuadragesimal voto en tus manos,
desengaño haré, corrector santo.

## IV ROMANCES

### I

(1580)

La más bella niña
de nuestro lugar,
hoy viuda y sola
y ayer por casar,
viendo que sus ojos 5
a la guerra van,
a su madre dice
que escucha su mal:
*Dejadme llorar*
*orillas del mar.* 10

Pues me distes, madre,
en tan tierna edad
tan corto el placer,
tan largo el pesar,
y me cautivastes 15
de quien hoy se va
y lleva las llaves
de mi libertad,
*dejadme llorar*
*orillas del mar.* 20

En llorar conviertan
mis ojos de hoy más
el sabroso oficio
del dulce mirar,
pues que no se pueden 25
mejor ocupar,
yéndose a la guerra
quien era mi paz.
*Dejadme llorar*
*orillas del mar.* 30

No me pongáis freno
ni queráis culpar,
que lo uno es justo,
lo otro por demás.
35 Si me queréis bien
no me hagáis mal;
harto peor fuera
morir y callar.
*Dejadme llorar*
40 *orillas del mar.*

Dulce madre mía,
¿quién no llorará
aunque tenga el pecho
como un pedernal
45 y no dará voces
viendo marchitar
los más verdes años
de mi mocedad?
*Dejadme llorar*
50 *orillas del mar.*

Váyanse las noches,
pues ido se han
los ojos que hacían
los míos velar;
55 váyanse y no vean
tanta soledad
después que en mi lecho
sobra la mitad.
*Dejadme llorar*
60 *orillas del mar.*

## 2

(1582)

*¡Que se nos va la pascua, mozas,*
*que se nos va la pascua!*

Mozuelas las de mi barrio,
loquillas y confiadas,
mirad no os engañe el tiempo, 5
la edad y la confïanza.
No os dejéis lisonjear
de la juventud lozana,
porque de caducas flores
teje el tiempo sus guirnaldas. 10
*¡Que se nos va la pascua, mozas,*
*que se nos va la pascua!*

Vuelan los ligeros años
y con presurosas alas
nos roban, como harpías, 15
nuestras sabrosas vïandas.
La flor de la maravilla
esta verdad nos declara,
porque le hurta la tarde
lo que le dio la mañana. 20
*¡Que se nos va la pascua, mozas,*
*que se nos va la pascua!*

Mirad que cuando pensáis
que hacen la señal de la alba
las campanas de la vida, 25
es la queda, y os desarma
de vuestro color y lustre,
de vuestro donaire y gracia,
y quedáis todas perdidas
por mayores de la marca. 30
*¡Que se nos va la pascua, mozas,*
*que se nos va la pascua!*

Yo sé de una buena vieja
que fue en un tiempo rubia y zarca,
35 y que al presente le cuesta
harto caro el ver su cara;
porque su bruñida frente
y sus mejillas se hallan
más que roquete de obispo
40 encogidas y arrugadas.
*¡Que se nos va la pascua, mozas,*
*que se nos va la pascua!*

Y sé de otra buena vieja
que un diente que le quedaba
45 se lo dejó estotro día
sepultado en unas natas;
y con lágrimas le dice:
'Diente mío de mi alma,
yo sé cuándo fuistes perla,
50 aunque ahora no sois nada.'
*¡Que se nos va la pascua, mozas,*
*que se nos va la pascua!*

Por eso, mozuelas locas
antes que la edad avara
55 el rubio cabello de oro
convierta en luciente plata,
quered cuando sois queridas,
amad cuando sois amadas;
mirad, bobas, que detrás
60 se pinta la ocasión calva.
*¡Que se nos va la pascua, mozas,*
*que se nos va la pascua!*

## 3

(1583)

Amarrado al duro banco
de una galera turquesca,
ambas manos en el remo
y ambos ojos en la tierra,

un forzado de Dragut 5
en la playa de Marbella
se quejaba al ronco son
del remo y de la cadena:
'¡Oh sagrado mar de España,
famosa playa serena, 10
teatro donde se han hecho
cien mil navales tragedias!
'Pues eres tú el mismo mar
que con tus crecientes besas
las murallas de mi patria, 15
coronadas y soberbias,
'tráeme nuevas de mi esposa,
y díme si han sido ciertas
las lágrimas y suspiros
que me dice por sus letras; 20
'porque si es verdad que llora
mi captiverio en tu arena,
bien puedes al mar del sur
vencer en lucientes perlas.
'Dáme ya, sagrado mar, 25
a mis demandas respuesta,
que bien puedes, si es verdad
que las aguas tienen lengua;
'pero, pues no me respondes,
sin duda alguna que es muerta, 30
aunque no lo debe ser,
pues que vivo yo en su ausencia.
'¡Pues he vivido diez años
sin libertad y sin ella,
siempre al remo condenado, 35
a nadie matarán penas!'
En esto se descubrieron
de la Religión seis velas,
y el cómitre mandó usar
al forzado de su fuerza. 40

## 4

(1584)

Noble desengaño,
gracias doy al cielo
que rompiste el lazo
que me tenía preso.
5 Por tan gran milagro
colgaré en tu templo
las graves cadenas
de mis graves yerros.
Las fuertes coyundas
10 del yugo de acero,
que con tu favor
sacudí del cuello,
las húmidas velas
y los rotos remos,
15 que escapé del mar
y ofrecí en el puerto,
ya de tus paredes
serán ornamento,
gloria de tu nombre,
20 y de Amor descuento.
Y así, pues que triunfas
del rapaz arquero,
tiren de tu carro
y sean tu trofeo
25 locas esperanzas,
vanos pensamientos,
pasos esparcidos,
livianos deseos,
rabiosos cuidados,
30 ponzoñosos celos,
infernales glorias,
gloriosos infiernos.
Compóngante himnos,
y digan sus versos
35 que libras captivos
y das vista a ciegos.

Ante tu deidad
hónrense mil fuegos
del sudor precioso
del árbol sabeo. 40
Pero ¿quién me mete
en cosas de seso,
y en hablar de veras
en aquestos tiempos,
donde el que más trata 45
de burlas y juegos,
ése es quien se viste
más a lo moderno?
Ingrata señora
de tus aposentos, 50
más dulce y sabrosa
que nabo en adviento,
aplícame un rato
el oído atento,
que quiero hacer auto 55
de mis devaneos.
¡Qué de noches frías
que me tuvo el hielo
tal, que por esquina
me juzgó tu perro, 60
y alzando la pierna,
con gentil denuedo,
me argentó de plata
los zapatos negros!
¡Qué de noches destas, 65
señora, me acuerdo
que andando a buscar
chinas por el suelo,
para hacer la seña
por el agujero, 70
al tomar la china
me ensucié los dedos!
¡Qué de días anduve
cargado de acero

75 con harto trabajo,
porque estaba enfermo!
Como estaba flaco,
parecía cencerro:
hierro por de fuera,
80 por de dentro hueso.
¡Qué de meses y años
que viví muriendo
en la Peña Pobre
sin ser Beltenebros;
85 donde me acaeció
mil días enteros
no comer sino uñas,
haciendo sonetos!
¡Qué de necedades
90 escribí en mil pliegos,
que las ríes tú ahora
y yo las confieso!
Aunque las tuvimos
ambos, en un tiempo,
95 yo por discreciones
y tú por requiebros.
¡Qué de medias noches
canté en mi instrumento:
'Socorred, señora,
100 con agua a mi fuego'!
Donde, aunque tú no
socorriste luego,
socorrió el vecino
con un gran caldero.
105 Adiós, mi señora,
porque me es tu gesto
chimenea en verano
y nieve en invierno,
y el bazo me tienes
110 de guijarros lleno,
porque creo que bastan
seis años de necio.

5

(1585)

Entre los sueltos caballos
de los vencidos cenetes,
que por el campo buscaban
entre la sangre lo verde,
aquel español de Orán 5
un suelto caballo prende,
por sus relinchos lozano
y por sus cernejas fuerte,
para que le lleve a él
y a un moro captivo lleve: 10
un moro que ha captivado,
capitán de cien jinetes.
En el ligero caballo
suben ambos, y él parece,
de cuatro espuelas herido, 15
que cuatro alas le mueven.
Triste camina el alarbe,
y lo más bajo que puede
ardientes suspiros lanza
y amargas lágrimas vierte. 20
Admirado el español
de ver cada vez que vuelve
que tan tiernamente llore
quien tan duramente hiere,
con razones le pregunta, 25
comedidas y corteses,
de sus suspiros la causa,
si la causa lo consiente.
El captivo, como tal,
sin excusas le obedece, 30
y a su piadosa demanda
satisface desta suerte:
'Valiente eres, capitán,
y cortés como valiente;
por tu espada y por tu trato 35
me has captivado dos veces.

Preguntado me has la causa
de mis suspiros ardientes
y débote la respuesta
40 por quien soy y por quien eres.
En los Gelves nací, el año
que os perdistes en los Gelves,
de una berberisca noble
y de un turco matasiete.
45 En Tremecén me crié
con mi madre y mis parientes
después que perdí a mi padre,
corsario de tres bajeles.
Junto a mi casa vivía,
50 porque más cerca muriese,
una dama de linaje
de los nobles Melioneses,
extremo de las hermosas,
cuando no de las crueles,
55 hija al fin destas arenas,
engendradoras de sierpes.
Cada vez que la miraba
salía un sol por su frente,
de tantos rayos ceñido
60 cuantos cabellos contiene.
Juntos así nos criamos,
y Amor en nuestras niñeces
hirió nuestros corazones
con arpones diferentes.
65 Labró el oro en mis entrañas
dulces lazos, tiernas redes,
mientras el plomo en las suyas
libertades y desdenes.
Apenas vide trocada
70 la dureza desta sierpe,
cuando tú me captivaste:
¡mira si es bien que lamente!'

## 6

(1587)

Servía en Orán al Rey
un español con dos lanzas,
y con el alma y la vida
a una gallarda africana,
tan noble como hermosa, 5
tan amante como amada,
con quien estaba una noche
cuando tocaron al arma.
Trecientos cenetes eran
de este rebato la causa, 10
que los rayos de la luna
descubrieron sus adargas;
las adargas avisaron
a las mudas atalayas,
las atalayas los fuegos, 15
los fuegos a las campanas;
y ellas al enamorado,
que en los brazos de su dama
oyó el militar estruendo
de las trompas y las cajas. 20
Espuelas de honor le pican
y freno de amor le para;
no salir es cobardía,
ingratitud es dejalla.
Del cuello pendiente ella, 25
viéndole tomar la espada,
con lágrimas y suspiros
le dice aquestas palabras:
'Salid al campo, señor,
bañen mis ojos la cama; 30
que ella me será también,
sin vos, campo de batalla.
Vestíos y salid apriesa,
que el general os aguarda;
yo os hago a vos mucha sobra 35
y vos a él mucha falta.

Bien podéis salir desnudo,
pues mi llanto no os ablanda;
que tenéis de acero el pecho
40 y no habéis menester armas.'
Viendo el español brioso
cuánto le detiene y habla,
le dice así: 'Mi señora,
tan dulce como enojada,
45 porque con honra y amor
yo me quede, cumpla y vaya,
vaya a los moros el cuerpo
y quede con vos el alma.
Concededme, dueño mío,
50 licencia para que salga
al rebato en vuestro nombre,
y en vuestro nombre combata.'

## 7

(1589)

*Leandro y Hero*

Arrojóse el mancebito
al charco de los atunes,
como si fuera el estrecho
poco más de medio azumbre.
5 Ya se va dejando atrás
las pedorreras azules
con que enamoró en Abido
mil mozuelas agridulces.
Del estrecho la mitad
10 pasaba sin pesadumbre,
los ojos en el candil,
que del fin temblando luce,
cuando el enemigo cielo
disparó sus arcabuces,
15 se desatacó la noche
y se orinaron las nubes.

Los vientos desenfrenados
parece que entonces huyen
del odre donde los tuvo
el griego de los embustes. 20
El fiero mar alterado,
que ya sufrió como yunque
al ejército de Jerjes,
hoy a un mozuelo no sufre.
Mas el animoso joven, 25
con los ojos cuando sube,
con el alma cuando baja,
siempre su norte descubre.
No hay ninfa de Vesta alguna
que así de su fuego cuide 30
como la dama de Sesto
cuida de guardar su lumbre.
Con las almenas la ampara,
porque ve lo que le cumple;
con las manos la defiende 35
y con las ropas la cubre.
Pero poco le aprovecha,
por más remedios que use,
que el viento con su esperanza
y con la llama concluye. 40
Ella, entonces, derramando
dos mil perlas de ambas luces,
a Venus y a Amor promete
sacrificios y perfumes.
Pero Amor, como llovía 45
y estaba en cueros, no acude,
ni Venus, porque con Marte
está cenando unas ubres.
El amador, en perdiendo
el farol que le conduce, 50
menos nada y más trabaja,
más teme y menos presume.
Ya tiene menos vigor,
ya más veces se zabulle,

55 ya ve en el agua la muerte,
ya se acaba, ya se hunde.
Apenas espiró, cuando,
bien fuera de su costumbre,
cuatro palanquines vientos
60 a la orilla le sacuden;
al pie de la amada torre
donde Hero se consume,
no deja estrella en el cielo
que no maldiga y acuse.
65 Y viendo el difunto cuerpo,
la vez que se lo descubren
de los relámpagos grandes
las temerosas vislumbres,
desde la alta torre envía
70 el cuerpo a su amante dulce,
y la alma adonde se queman
pastillas de piedra zufre.
Apenas del mar salía
el Sol a rayar las cumbres,
75 cuando la doncella de Hero,
temiendo el suceso, acude;
y viendo hecha pedazos
aquella flor de virtudes,
de cada ojo derrama
80 de lágrimas dos almudes.
Juntando los mal logrados,
con un punzón de un estuche
hizo que estas tristes letras
una blanca piedra ocupen:
85 'Hero somos y Leandro,
no menos necios que ilustres,
en amores y firmezas
al mundo ejemplos comunes.
El Amor, como dos huevos,
90 quebrantó nuestras saludes;
él fue pasado por agua,
yo estrellada mi fin tuve.

Rogamos a nuestros padres
que no se pongan capuces;
sino, pues un fin tuvimos, 95
que una tierra nos sepulte.'

## 8

(1590)

Lloraba la niña
(y tenía razón)
la prolija ausencia
de su ingrato amor.
Dejóla tan niña, 5
que apenas creo yo
que tenía los años
que ha que la dejó.
Llorando la ausencia
del galán traidor, 10
la halla la luna
y la deja el sol,
añadiendo siempre
pasión a pasión,
memoria a memoria, 15
dolor a dolor.
*Llorad, corazón,*
*que tenéis razón.*

Dícele su madre:
'Hija, por mi amor 20
que se acabe el llanto,
o me acabe yo.'
Ella le responde:
'No podrá ser, no:
las causas son muchas, 25
los ojos son dos.
Satisfagan, madre,
tanta sinrazón,
y lágrimas lloren
en esta ocasión 30

tantas como dellos
un tiempo tiró
flechas amorosas
el arquero dios.
35 Ya no canto, madre,
y si canto yo,
muy tristes endechas
mis canciones son;
porque el que se fue,
40 con lo que llevó,
se dejó el silencio,
y llevó la voz.'
*Llorad, corazón,*
*que tenéis razón.*

## 9

(1602)

### *Angélica y Medoro*

En un pastoral albergue,
que la guerra entre unos robres
le dejó por escondido
o le perdonó por pobre,
5 do la paz viste pellico
y conduce entre pastores
ovejas del monte al llano
y cabras del llano al monte,
mal herido y bien curado,
10 se alberga un dichoso joven,
que sin clavarle Amor flecha
le coronó de favores.
Las venas con poca sangre,
los ojos con mucha noche
15 le halló en el campo aquella
vida y muerte de los hombres.
Del palafrén se derriba,
no porque al moro conoce,
sino por ver que la hierba

tanta sangre paga en flores. 20
Límpiale el rostro, y la mano
siente al Amor que se esconde
tras las rosas, que la muerte
va violando sus colores.
Escondióse tras las rosas 25
porque labren sus arpones
el diamante del Catay
con aquella sangre noble.
Ya le regala los ojos,
ya le entra, sin ver por dónde, 30
una piedad mal nacida
entre dulces escorpiones.
Ya es herido el pedernal,
ya despide el primer golpe
centellas de agua. ¡Oh, piedad, 35
hija de padres traidores!
Hierbas aplica a sus llagas,
que si no sanan entonces,
en virtud de tales manos
lisonjean los dolores. 40
Amor le ofrece su venda,
mas ella sus velos rompe
para ligar sus heridas:
los rayos del sol perdonen.
Los últimos nudos daba 45
cuando el cielo la socorre
de un villano en una yegua
que iba penetrando el bosque.
Enfrénanle de la bella
las tristes piadosas voces, 50
que los firmes troncos mueven
y las sordas piedras oyen;
y la que mejor se halla
en las selvas que en la corte
simple bondad al pío ruego 55
cortésmente corresponde.
Humilde se apea el villano

y sobre la yegua pone
un cuerpo con poca sangre,
60 pero con dos corazones;
a su cabaña los guía,
que el sol deja su horizonte
y el humo de su cabaña
les va sirviendo de norte.
65 Llegaron temprano a ella,
do una labradora acoge
un mal vivo con dos almas
y una ciega con dos soles.
Blando heno en vez de pluma
70 para lecho les compone,
que será tálamo luego
do el garzón sus dichas logre.
Las manos, pues, cuyos dedos
desta vida fueron dioses,
75 restituyen a Medoro
salud nueva, fuerzas dobles,
y le entregan, cuando menos,
su beldad y un reino en dote,
segunda invidia de Marte,
80 primera dicha de Adonis.
Corona un lascivo enjambre
de Cupidillos menores
la choza, bien como abejas
hueco tronco de alcornoque.
85 ¡Qué de nudos le está dando
a un áspid la invidia torpe,
contando de las palomas
los arrullos gemidores!
¡Qué bien la destierra Amor,
90 haciendo la cuerda azote,
porque el caso no se infame
y el lugar no se inficione!
Todo es gala el africano,
su vestido espira olores,
95 el lunado arco suspende,

y el corvo alfanje depone.
  Tórtolas enamoradas
son sus roncos atambores,
y los volantes de Venus
sus bien seguidos pendones. 100
  Desnuda el pecho anda ella,
vuela el cabello sin orden;
si le abrocha, es con claveles,
con jazmines si le coge.
  El pie calza en lazos de oro, 105
porque la nieve se goce,
y no se vaya por pies
la hermosura del orbe.
  Todo sirve a los amantes:
plumas les baten, veloces, 110
airecillos lisonjeros,
si no son murmuradores.
  Los campos les dan alfombras,
los árboles pabellones,
la apacible fuente sueño, 115
música los ruiseñores.
  Los troncos les dan cortezas
en que se guarden sus nombres,
mejor que en tablas de mármol
o que en láminas de bronce. 120
  No hay verde fresno sin letra,
ni blanco chopo sin mote;
si un valle 'Angélica' suena,
otro 'Angélica' responde.
  Cuevas do el silencio apenas 125
deja que sombras las moren
profanan con sus abrazos
a pesar de sus horrores.
  Choza, pues, tálamo y lecho,
cortesanos labradores, 130
aires, campos, fuentes, vegas,
cuevas, troncos, aves, flores,
  fresnos, chopos, montes, valles,

contestes de estos amores,
135 el cielo os guarde, si puede,
de las locuras del Conde.

## 10

(1603)

En los pinares de Júcar
vi bailar unas serranas,
al son del agua en las piedras
y al son del viento en las ramas.
5 No es blanco coro de ninfas
de las que aposenta el agua
o las que venera el bosque,
seguidoras de Diana:
serranas eran de Cuenca,
10 honor de aquella montaña,
cuyo pie besan dos ríos
por besar de ella las plantas.
Alegres corros tejían,
dándose las manos blancas
15 de amistad, quizá temiendo
no la truequen las mudanzas.
*¡Qué bien bailan las serranas!*
*¡Qué bien bailan!*

El cabello en crespos nudos
20 luz da al sol, oro a la Arabia,
cuál de flores impedido,
cuál de cordones de plata.
Del color visten del cielo,
si no son de la esperanza,
25 palmillas que menosprecian
al zafiro y la esmeralda.
El pie (cuando lo permite
la brújula de la falda)
lazos calza, y mirar deja
30 pedazos de nieve y nácar.

Ellas, cuyo movimiento
honestamente levanta
el cristal de la columna
sobre la pequeña basa,—
*¡qué bien bailan las serranas!* 35
*¡Qué bien bailan!*

Una entre los blancos dedos
hiriendo negras pizarras,
instrumento de marfil
que las musas le invidiaran, 40
las aves enmudeció,
y enfrenó el curso del agua;
no se movieron las hojas,
por no impedir lo que canta:
'Serranas de Cuenca 45
iban al pinar,
*unas por piñones,*
*otras por bailar.*

Bailando y partiendo
las serranas bellas 50
un piñón con otro,
si ya no es con perlas,
de Amor las saetas
huelgan de trocar,
*unas por piñones,* 55
*otras por bailar.*

Entre rama y rama,
cuando el ciego dios
pide al sol los ojos
por verlas mejor, 60
los ojos del sol
las veréis pisar,
*unas por piñones,*
*otras por bailar.*'

## II

(1608)

Las flores del romero,
niña Isabel,
*hoy son flores azules,*
*mañana serán miel.*

5 Celosa estás, la niña,
celosa estás de aquel
dichoso, pues le buscas,
ciego, pues no te ve,
ingrato, pues te enoja
10 y confiado, pues
no se disculpa hoy
de lo que hizo ayer.
Enjuguen esperanzas
lo que lloras por él;
15 que celos entre aquellos
que se han querido bien
*hoy son flores azules,*
*mañana serán miel.*

Aurora de ti misma,
20 que cuando a amanecer
a tu placer empiezas,
te eclipsan tu placer,
serénense tus ojos,
y más perlas no des,
25 porque al sol le está mal
lo que a la aurora bien.
Desata como nieblas
todo lo que no ves;
que sospechas de amantes
30 y querellas después
*hoy son flores azules,*
*mañana serán miel.*

## 12

(1609)

*Del Palacio de la Primavera*

Esperando están la rosa
cuantas contiene un vergel
flores, hijas de la aurora,
bellas cuanto pueden ser.
Ella, aunque con majestad, 5
no debajo de dosel,
sino sobre alfombras verdes,
purpúrea se dejó ver.
Como a reina de las flores,
guarda la ciñe fïel, 10
si son archas las espinas
que en torno de ella se ven.
Al aparecer la hicieron
una inclinación cortés,
y con muy buen aire todas, 15
que mal pudieran sin él.
No la hicieron reverencia,
aunque todas tienen pies,
porque su inmovilidad
su mayor disculpa fué. 20
El vulgo de esotras hierbas,
sirviéndoles esta vez
de verdes lenguas sus hojas,
la saludaron también.
Quién pretende la privanza 25
de tan gran señora, y quién,
admirando su beldad,
no osa descubrir su fe;
que el Cupido de las flores
es la abeja y, si lo es, 30
sus flechas abrevia todas
en el aguijón cruel.
Ella, pues, las solicita,
y las despoja después;

35 por señas que sus despojos
son dulces como la miel.
Los colores de la reina
vistió galán el clavel,
príncipe que es de la sangre,
40 y aun aspirante a ser rey.
En viéndola, dijo '¡ay!'
el jacinto, y al papel
lo encomendó de sus hojas
porque se pueda leer.
45 Ámbar espira el vestido
del blanco jazmín, de aquél
cuya castidad lasciva
Venus hipócrita es.
La fuente deja el narciso,
50 que no es poco para él,
y ya no se mira a sí,
admirando lo que ve.
¡Oh, qué celoso está el lilio,
un mal cortesano que
55 calza siempre borceguí:
debe de ser portugués!
Mosquetas y clavellinas
sus damas son. ¿Qué más quiés,
oh tú que pides lugar,
60 que bel mirar y oler bien?
Las azucenas la sirven
de dueñas de honor, y a fe
que sus diez varas de holanda
las invidian más de diez.
65 Meninas son las violetas,
y muy bien lo pueden ser
las primicias de las flores,
que antes huelen que se ven.
De este real paraíso,
70 verde jaula es un laurel
de tres dulces ruiseñores
que cantan a dos y a tres.

Guardadamas es un triste
fruncidísimo ciprés,
efecto al fin de su fruta, 75
para lo que yo me sé.
Bufones son los estanques,
y en qué lo son lo diré:
en lo frío lo primero
que se me ha de conceder; 80
en el murmurar continuo
y en el reírse también,
aunque hacen poco ruido,
con ser hombres de placer;
en el pedir, y no agua, 85
que no es de agua su interés,
ni piden lo que no beben,
por siempre jamás, Amén.
Este de la primavera
el verde palacio es, 90
que cada año se erige
para poco más de un mes.
Las flores a las personas
ciertos ejemplos les den:
que puede ser yermo hoy 95
el que fue jardín ayer.

## 13

(1620)

*Al Nacimiento de Cristo Nuestro Señor*

Cuantos silbos, cuantas voces
tus campos, Bethlén, oyeron,
sentidas bien de sus valles,
guardadas mal de sus ecos,
pastores las dan, buscando 5
el que, celestial Cordero,
nos abrió piadoso el libro
que negaban tantos sellos.

*¡Qué buscáis, los ganaderos!*<br>
10 *— Uno, ay, niño, que su cuna*<br>
*los brazos son de la Luna,*<br>
*si duermen sus dos luceros.*

No pastor, no abrigó fiera<br>
frágil choza, albergue ciego,<br>
15 que no penetre el cuidado,<br>
que no escudriñe el deseo.<br>
La diligencia, calzada<br>
en vez de abarcas el viento,<br>
cumbres pisa coronadas<br>
20 de paraninfos del cielo.<br>
*¡Qué buscáis, los ganaderos!*<br>
*— Uno, ay, niño, que su cuna*<br>
*los brazos son de la Luna,*<br>
*si duermen sus dos luceros.*<br>
25 *— Pediros albricias puedo.*<br>
PASTORES *¿De qué, Gil?*<br>
GIL *No deis más paso;*<br>
*que dormir vi al niño.*<br>
PASTORES *¡Paso,*<br>
*quedo ¡ay! queditico, quedo!*

Tanto he visto celestial,<br>
30 tan luminoso, tan raro,<br>
que a pesar, hallarás claro,<br>
de la noche, este portal.<br>
Enfrena el paso, Pascual,<br>
deja a la puerta el denuedo.<br>
35 *— Pediros albricias puedo.*<br>
PASTORES *¿De qué, Gil?*<br>
GIL *No deis más paso;*<br>
*que dormir vi al niño.*<br>
PASTORES *¡Paso,*<br>
*quedo ¡ay! queditico, quedo!*

## 14

(1621)

Guarda corderos, zagala,
zagala, no guardes fe;
que quien te hizo pastora
no te excusó de mujer.
La pureza del armiño, 5
que tan celebrada es,
vístela con el pellico
y desnúdala con él.
Deja a las piedras lo firme,
advirtiendo que tal vez, 10
a pesar de su dureza,
obedecen al cincel.
Resiste al viento la encina,
mas con el villano pie;
que con las hojas corteses 15
a cualquier céfiro cree.
Aquella hermosa vid
que abrazada al olmo ves
parte pámpanos, discreta,
con el vecino laurel. 20
Tortolilla gemidora,
depuesto el casto desdén,
tálamo hizo segundo
los ramos de aquel ciprés.
No para una abeja sola 25
sus hojas guarda el clavel,
beben otras el aljófar
que borda su rosicler.
El cristal de aquel arroyo,
undosamente fïel, 30
niega al ausente su imagen
hasta que le vuelve a ver.
La inconstancia al fin da plumas
al hijo de Venus, que
poblando dellas sus alas, 35
viste sus flechas también.

No, pues, tu libre albedrío
lo tiranice interés,
ni amor que de singular
40 tenga más que de infïel.
Sacude preciosos yugos,
coyundas de oro no den,
sino cordones de lana,
al suelto cabello ley.
45 Mal hayas tú si constante
mirares al sol, y quien
tan águila fuere en esto,
dos veces mal haya y tres.
Mal hayas tú si imitares,
50 en lasciva candidez,
las aves de la deidad
que primero espuma fue.
Solicitando prolija
la ingratitud de un doncel,
55 ninfa de las selvas ya
vocal sombra vino a ser.
Si quieres, pues, zagaleja,
de tu hermosura cruel
dar entera voz al valle,
60 desprecia mi parecer.

## V 'LETRILLAS'

### I

(1581)

*Ándeme yo caliente*
*y ríase la gente.*
Traten otros del gobierno
del mundo y sus monarquías,
mientras gobiernan mis días 5
mantequillas y pan tierno,
y las mañanas de invierno
naranjada y aguardiente,
*y ríase la gente.*

Coma en dorada vajilla 10
el príncipe mil cuidados,
como píldoras dorados;
que yo en mi pobre mesilla
quiero más una morcilla
que en el asador reviente, 15
*y ríase la gente.*

Cuando cubra las montañas
de blanca nieve el enero,
tenga yo lleno el brasero
de bellotas y castañas, 20
y quien las dulces patrañas
del Rey que rabió me cuente,
*y ríase la gente.*

Busque muy en hora buena
el mercader nuevos soles; 25
yo conchas y caracoles
entre la menuda arena,
escuchando a Filomena
sobre el chopo de la fuente,
*y ríase la gente.* 30

Pase a media noche el mar,
y arda en amorosa llama
Leandro por ver su Dama;
que yo más quiero pasar
35 del golfo de mi lagar
la blanca o roja corriente,
*y ríase la gente.*

Pues Amor es tan cruel,
que de Píramo y su amada
40 hace tálamo una espada,
do se junten ella y él,
sea mi Tisbe un pastel,
y la espada sea mi diente,
*y ríase la gente.*

## 2

(1581)

Da bienes Fortuna
que no están escritos:
*cuando pitos flautas,*
*cuando flautas pitos.*

5 ¡Cuán diversas sendas
se suelen seguir
en el repartir
honras y haciendas!
A unos da encomiendas,
10 a otros sambenitos.
*Cuando pitos flautas,*
*cuando flautas pitos.*

A veces despoja
de choza y apero
15 al mayor cabrero;
y a quien se le antoja
la cabra más coja
pare dos cabritos.
*Cuando pitos flautas,*
20 *cuando flautas pitos.*

En gustos de amores
suele traer bonanza
y en breve mudanza
los vuelve en dolores.
No da a uno favores, 25
y a otro infinitos.
*Cuando pitos flautas,*
*cuando flautas pitos.*

Porque en una aldea
un pobre mancebo 30
hurtó sólo un huevo,
al sol bambolea;
y otro se pasea
con cien mil delitos.
*Cuando pitos flautas,* 35
*cuando flautas pitos.*

## 3

(1609)

*No son todos ruiseñores*
*los que cantan entre las flores,*
*sino campanitas de plata,*
*que tocan a la alba;*
*sino trompeticas de oro,* 5
*que hacen la salva*
*a los soles que adoro.*

No todas las voces ledas
son de sirenas con plumas,
cuyas húmidas espumas 10
son las verdes alamedas.
Si suspendido te quedas
a los suaves clamores,
*no son todos ruiseñores*
*los que cantan entre las flores,* 15
*sino campanitas de plata,*
*que tocan a la alba;*

*sino trompeticas de oro,*
*que hacen la salva*
20 *a los soles que adoro.*

Lo artificioso que admira,
y lo dulce que consuela,
no es de aquel violín que vuela
ni de esotra inquieta lira;
25 otro instrumento es quien tira
de los sentidos mejores:
*no son todos ruiseñores*
*los que cantan entre las flores,*
*sino campanitas de plata,*
30 *que tocan a la alba,*
*sino trompeticas de oro*
*que hacen la salva*
*a los soles que adoro.*

Las campanitas lucientes,
35 y los dorados clarines
en coronados jazmines,
los dos hermosos corrientes
no sólo recuerdan gentes
sino convocan amores.
40 *No son todos ruiseñores*
*los que cantan entre las flores,*
*sino campanitas de plata,*
*que tocan a la alba,*
*sino trompeticas de oro,*
45 *que hacen la salva*
*a los soles que adoro.*

## 4

(1620)

*Ánsares de Menga*
*al arroyo van:*
*ellos visten nieve,*
*él corre cristal.*

El arroyo espera 5
las hermosas aves,
que cisnes süaves
son de su ribera;
cuya Venus era
hija de Pascual. 10
*Ellos visten nieve,*
*él corre cristal.*

Pudiera la pluma
del menos bizarro
conducir el carro 15
de la que fue espuma;
en beldad, no en suma,
lucido caudal.
*Ellos visten nieve,*
*él corre cristal.* 20

Trenzado el cabello
los sigue Minguilla,
y en la verde orilla,
desnuda el pie bello,
granjeando en ello 25
marfil oriental
*los que visten nieve,*
*quien corre cristal.*

La agua apenas trata
cuando dirás que 30
se desata el pie,
y no se desata,
plata dando a plata
con que, liberal
*los viste de nieve,* 35
*le presta cristal.*

## 5

(1621)

### *Al nacimiento de Cristo Nuestro Señor*

*Caído se le ha un clavel*
*hoy a la Aurora del seno:*
*¡qué glorioso que está el heno,*
*porque ha caído sobre él!*

5 Cuando el silencio tenía
todas las cosas del suelo,
y coronada del yelo
reinaba la noche fría,
en medio la monarquía
10 de tiniebla tan crüel,
*caído se le ha un clavel*
*hoy a la Aurora del seno:*
*¡qué glorioso que está el heno,*
*porque ha caído sobre él!*

15 De un solo clavel ceñida
la Virgen, Aurora bella,
al mundo se lo dio, y ella
quedó cual antes florida;
a la púrpura caída
20 solo fue el heno fïel.
*Caído se le ha un clavel*
*hoy a la Aurora del seno:*
*¡qué glorioso que está el heno,*
*porque ha caído sobre él!*

25 El heno, pues, que fue dino,
a pesar de tantas nieves,
de ver en sus brazos leves
este rosicler divino
para su lecho fue lino,
30 oro para su dosel.
*Caído se le ha un clavel*
*hoy a la aurora del seno:*
*¡qué glorioso que está el heno,*
*porque ha caído sobre él!*

## 6

(1621)

*Aprended, Flores, de mi*
*lo que va de ayer a hoy,*
*que ayer maravilla fui,*
*y hoy sombra mía aun no soy.*

La Aurora ayer me dio cuna, 5
la noche ataúd me dio;
sin luz muriera si no
me la prestara la luna:
pues de vosotras ninguna
deja de acabar así, 10
*aprended, Flores, de mí*
*lo que va de ayer a hoy,*
*que ayer maravilla fui,*
*y hoy sombra mía aun no soy.*

Consuelo dulce el clavel 15
es a la breve edad mía,
pues quien me concedió un día,
dos apenas le dio a él:
efímeras del vergel
yo cárdena, él carmesí. 20
*Aprended, Flores, de mí*
*lo que va de ayer a hoy,*
*que ayer maravilla fui,*
*y hoy sombra mía aun no soy.*

Flor es el jazmín, si bella, 25
no de las más vividoras,
pues dura pocas más horas
que rayos tiene de estrella;
si el ámbar florece, es ella
la flor que él retiene en sí. 30
*Aprended, Flores, de mí*
*lo que va de ayer a hoy,*
*que ayer maravilla fui,*
*y hoy sombra mía aun no soy.*

35 El alhelí, aunque grosero
en fragancia y en color,
más días ve que otra flor,
pues ve los de un mayo entero:
morir maravilla quiero
40 y no vivir alhelí.
*Aprended, Flores de mí*
*lo que va de ayer a hoy,*
*que ayer maravilla fui,*
*y hoy sombra mía aun no soy.*

45 A ninguna flor mayores
términos concede el Sol
que al sublime girasol,
Matusalén de las flores:
ojos son aduladores
50 cuantas en él hojas vi.
*Aprended, Flores, de mí*
*lo que va de ayer a hoy,*
*que ayer maravilla fui,*
*y hoy sombra mía aun no soy.*

## VI 'DÉCIMAS'

(1603)

De un monte en los senos, donde
daba un tronco entre unas peñas
dulces sonorosas señas
de los cristales que esconde,
5 Eco, que al latir responde
del sabueso diligente,
condujo, perlas su frente,
fatigada cazadora,
que blancos lilios fue un hora,
10 a las orlas de la fuente.

*Montaña que, eminente,*
*al viento tus encinas*
*sonantes cuernos son, roncas bocinas;*
*toca, toca, toca,*
*monteros convoca* 15
*tras la blanca cierva,*
*que sudando aljófar*
*corona la yerba.*

Treguas poniendo al calor,
lisonjean su fatiga, 20
no sé cuáles plumas diga,
del Céfiro o del Amor;
no a blanca o purpúrea flor
abeja más diligente
liba el rocío luciente, 25
que las dos alas, sin verlas,
desvanecieron las perlas
que invidia el nácar de Oriente.

*Montaña que, eminente,*
*al viento tus encinas* 30
*sonantes cuernos son, roncas bocinas;*
*toca, toca, toca,*
*monteros convoca*
*tras la blanca cierva,*
*que sudando aljófar* 35
*corona la yerba.*

De Clori bebe el oído
el son del agua risueño,
y al instrumento del sueño
cuerdas ministra el ruido; 40
duerme, y Narciso Cupido,
cuando más está pendiente
(no sobre el cristal corriente)
sobre el dormido cristal,
fiera rompiendo el jaral, 45
rompe el sueño juntamente.

*Montaña que, eminente,*
*al viento tus encinas*
*sonantes cuernos son, roncas bocinas;*
50 *toca, toca, toca,*
*monteros convoca*
*tras la blanca cierva,*
*que sudando aljófar*
*corona la yerba.*

# NOTES ON THE POEMS

## I 'SOLEDAD PRIMERA'

*Dedication*

1–2. The construction is: *cuantos versos me dictó dulce musa son pasos de un peregrino errante*, 'These lines, dictated by the Muse, are the record of the footsteps of a wanderer'.

3–4. 'Some inspired, others straying in a confused wilderness.'

5. *impedido:* a Latinism, 'burdened'.

8. The mountains seem to threaten the sky like the Titans who rebelled against their father the Sky.

10–11. I.e. *que, muertas, pidiendo al teñido suelo términos disformes...:* the dead animals are so many that they seem to strain the natural bounds of the bloodstained (*teñido*) earth.

13. *arrima...fresno:* 'lean your spear (of ash) against the ash'.

15. *purpurear:* 'turn crimson'. *Púrpura* is not our purple.

16–21. An allusion to the hanging of trophies of the hunt on trees: 'while the huntsman diligently hangs on [*da al...*] the rugged oak [*robre = roble*] and on the lofty pine—living rivals of the crags in their height [and their strength?]—the terrible tokens [of the hunt: the head] of the bear which, though pierced through, still kissed the shaft of your shining spear' (i.e. as if in homage to the Duke).

22–5. I.e. *o lo sagrado de la encina supla lo augusto del dosel; o la alta zanefa (= cenefa) de la fuente [supla] lo majestuoso del sitïal debido a tu deidad:* 'whether the sacred ilex provide you with an august canopy or the bank of a stream take the place of your majestic seat of honour'.

29. I.e. *el césped no desnudo de grama.*

30–1. Note the antithetic *pie acertado/errantes pasos*: the poet has dedicated his uncertain steps (his halting verse) to the Duke so that in that, at least, his *pie* is *acertado.*

32. *cadena:* a feature of the Duke's coat of arms.

33–4. I.e. [*que este*] *süave, generoso nudo* (the *cadena* of 32) *honre* [*mi*] *libertad, perseguida de fortuna.* Góngora hopes to exchange indigent freedom for the generous patronage of the Duke, whose *cadena* stands for the vassalage the poet will gladly accept.

35–7. Euterpe (the Muse of flutes, but here taken to represent lyric inspiration) will in gratitude sing the Duke's praises (*dará su canoro instrumento al viento*) even if the trumpet of Fame be silent. That is, she will praise the Duke through Góngora's lyric poetry.

*Soledad Primera*

1–6. It is the season when Taurus seems to graze on stars in fields of sapphire: i.e. when the sun is in Taurus (which it enters about 21 April). *Mentido robador de Europa* alludes to Jupiter who (belying his true form, hence *mentido*) took the form of a bull in order to abduct Europa. Taurus is a celestial bull so his horns resemble the moon and his hide is as if made of sunbeams. Góngora's intricately involved circumlocution is not just idle decoration but a means of giving a mythical cast to the events his poetry describes. Jupiter is alluded to again in 8 and 28: it is probable that his astrological significance—benign, 'jovial', bringer of happiness—is being invoked to introduce the theme of the poem, and to preside over it.

7–8. The shipwrecked youth, more fitting to be the cupbearer of the gods than Ganymede, carried off by Jupiter from Mount Ida.

9–11. I.e. [the lovesick stranger] [*no solo*] *ausente* [*sino*] *náufrago y desdeñado, da dulces querellas lagrimosas al mar.*

11–14. *condolido* qualifies *mar*; the subject of *fue*... *fue* is *gemido.*

14. Arion was saved from drowning by dolphins attracted by his skill on the lyre: the youth's laments are like a second instrument of Arion in that they move sea and wind to similar compassion.

15–17. I.e. *breve tabla—piadoso miembro roto del pino siempre opuesto en la montaña al enemigo Noto* (the South wind) *no fue pequeño delfín:* the plank played the part of Arion's dolphin.

22–3. See p. 25.

24–5. The crag is crowned with an eagle's eyrie, made of *secos juncos* and *calientes plumas.*

26. The youth emerges from the sea covered with seaweed and foam.

28. The eagle, sacred to Jupiter.

29–31. I.e. *dio a la roca aquella parte poca de la rota nave que le expuso en la playa:* he offers to the rock, as a token of gratitude, the plank which brought him ashore.

34–6. I.e. *cuanto Océano ha bebido el vestido, le hace restituir a las arenas:* he wrings on to the sand all the sea-water his clothes have absorbed.

40–1. '[The sun] sucks the slightest trace of the Ocean's waves from the garments, even from their smallest thread.'

42–51. 'Scarcely did he see the horizons—which confusedly made mountains of water and seas of mountains—bereft of their light when the unfortunate stranger, putting on (*entregado en*) the clothes he had rescued from the fierce sea, treading twilight amid thorns, scaled—less tired than bewildered—crags that even a fleet, intrepid bird would only with difficulty surmount.'

53–5. The crag stands like a wall between sea and countryside, *árbitro igual* because it dominates impartially both *el mar siempre sonante* [*y*] *la muda campaña*: a beautifully expressed antithesis.

57. *declina al:* 'descends towards'.

60. *ferro:* 'anchor'.

62–4. The wanderer hopes that the light promises safety, *término luminoso de mi fortuna* ('vicissitudes'), like St Elmo's fire (thought by the ancients to indicate the presence and protection of Castor and Pollux, sons of Leda).

64–7. 'Fearing lest some envious and uncouth grove interpose itself between him and the light (making him lose his way), even if some conspiracy of the winds does not blow it out.'

68–76. I.e. *cual sigue el villano...aquella piedra, indigna tiara...de animal tenebroso....* The animal may be a tiger or a stag who, according to medieval tradition, bore in their head a precious stone that shone by night (so that their brow can fittingly be called a *carro brillante de nocturno día*, a bearer of light amidst the darkness). *Indigna* is a transferred epithet: the animal is undeserving of its bright jewel.

79–80. 'Traversing the rough as easily as the smooth.'

81–2. 'Making straight for the fire [shining like a ruby] as if it were the Pole-star of his compass [*aguja*: "compass-needle"]'.

83. *o...o:* 'whether...or'.

85. *convoca, despidiendo:* a good instance of Góngora's skill in compression of meaning: 'summons (by indicating where the goatherds are) while intending to scare away'.

86–9. 'The fire that from a distance seemed small proves, when close, to be so big that in it lies an entire sturdy oak, consumed (*desatada en cenizas*) like a butterfly burning in a candle-flame.' Góngora makes here no distinction between butterfly and moth.

90–2. I.e. *fue saludado de los conducidores de cabras* (the goatherds).

93. The goatherds sit in a circle round the fire, sacred to Vulcan. Góngora uses *coronar* on a number of occasions to mean 'surround', 'girdle'. Cf. Latin *corona*, a group of onlookers.

96. *Pales:* god of flocks and herds; *Flora:* goddess of flowering plants.

97–100. 'Modern artifice did not draft designs or sketch models (for the cottage), aspiring to make the sublime edifice fill the vault of heaven.'

109. *hidrópica de viento:* 'thirsty [as with dropsy] for empty honours'.

110–11. 'Envy, who feeds on the Egyptian asp'—traditionally associated with envy.

114. What this prattling (*bachillera*) Sphinx is remains uncertain: perhaps the frivolity and pleasure-seeking (or the flattery) of court life which makes the modern Narcissus (the courtier) seek echoes (empty pleasures, or flattery) and despise springs (of truth), unlike the Narcissus of myth.

117–19. I.e. *la ceremonia profana que gasta en salvas impertinentes la pólvora del tiempo más preciso:* 'worldly ceremonial which wastes in pointless salvoes the powder of most necessary time': useless ceremony wastes time as salvoes waste powder.

120–1. Courtly ceremonial is mocked by rustic sincerity, personified as a peasant leaning on a crook.

125–7. Flattery has lured many to destruction, as the Sirens lured ships of old.

128. Another line that illustrates Góngora's genius for compression —and beauty: 'trophies (victims) of an illusion, a sweet-sounding dream'. *Dulces* seems to be a transferred epithet: the trophies are made to reflect the sweetness of the *canoro sueño.*

129–31. A reference to the peacock, of beautiful plumage but ugly feet, hence a symbol of vanity. The image is a Golden Age commonplace, often used by Góngora himself, as in these lines: 'lying tongues do not here flatter the powerful and proud, as if beautifying the ugly feet of a peacock spreading its gorgeous tail'.

132–3. An allusion to Icarus. Favour at court is precarious: one lifted up today may be cast down tomorrow, falling into oblivion as Icarus fell to his death in the waves when the sun, which he had approached too nearly, melted the wax which held on his wings.

140–2. The goatherds show the same generosity as was to be found in the innocence (*candor*) of the Golden Age of Saturn, when men were content to dwell in woods and fields, and take trees as their shelter (*tienda*) and acorns as their food. Here *que = a quien.*

147–9. The milk (or, more likely, curds) given to the wanderer was milked at dawn, and so white that 'the lily-whiteness of the lovely brow of Dawn could not compare with it (*perdían con ella*)'.

152. Alcimedon was the inventor of the spoon, according to Virgil, *Eclogue* 3.

153–4. I.e. *el que fue esposo de doscientas cabras durante casi un lustro:* the leader of the herd for nearly five years.

161. The old billy-goat is now *cecina,* dried meat.

163–6. I.e. *pieles blandas le* ('for him') *solicitan más regalado sueño que púrpura tiria o milanés brocado* [*le solicitan*] *al príncipe entre holandas* ('lying between fine linen sheets').

167–70. The sense appears to be: 'In sleep, unaffected by heady wines, he does not dream vain dreams of grandeur that will leave him cheated when he wakes—like Sisyphus, for ever pushing uphill a stone that will always slip from his grasp and roll down again.'

173–5. He is awakened only by innocent rural sounds, such as the dog 'barking furiously at the dry leaf torn by the wind from an oak'.

177. The singing birds are like the sound of 'sweet bells of melodious

feathers', summoning the sun to rise and be about his duties: *esquila* is a small monastery bell that summons the inmates to their devotions.

190–1. 'His footsteps slowing in obedience to the many sights that the view presents.'

194–6. 'If the limited vista still covers much ground, much more is that which the sun veils with mist and distance conceals.'

204–5. *animal de Amaltea:* the goat Amalthea who suckled Zeus and whose horn is the horn of plenty; *si al animal...diáfanos cristales:* 'if it can be said that the crystal waters of a river are like the horns with which Amalthea was armed'.

206. *engazar = engarzar.*

210. *los jaspes líquidos:* the sea.

224–5. I.e. *que traía a las personas...si no* [*traía*] *precipitados los cerros....:* 'the torrent of the hunt seemed to drag people along with it, if not the very hills themselves'.

229. *reduciendo:* 'leading back'.

230–2. The goatherd 'speedily joins the hunt, increasing their number and adding his voice to the clamour'.

234–5. The goatherd, once a warrior, seems to mingle the attributes of Pan and Mars: in him Pan can be imagined armed, or Mars goat-footed.

237. *rémora:* the remora or sucking fish was thought capable of stopping a ship in full sail. Here the wanderer is stopped by the sound of music, as if his ear were a remora.

242. *cuando no:* 'even if not'.

244–5. I.e. *juntaba el líquido cristal* (the stream) *al humano* [*cristal*] (her white-skinned body), etc.: she cupped her hand to drink.

246. Her hand, whiter than the crystal of the stream, equals in whiteness the rest of her (*humano cristal*).

250. *si...no:* the construction expresses equivalence not antithesis here (see p. 8): the flowers in the girl's hair are the colours of dawn, while her hair is golden like the sun: 'if she is not like the dawn with golden beams, then she is like a sun with the colours of dawn'.

256–7. *lasciva...honesta:* a Greek accusative (see p. 7).

261–2. I.e. *ser menos las verdes Hamadrías que abortaron las plantas.* Each tree had its Hamadryad; the *serranas* seem to outnumber them.

267–70. 'Hidden in the hollow of an ilex, the youth feeds his eyes with beauty and his ear with music': he looks and listens avidly.

271–4. I.e. [*El joven*] *buscaba el Sileno de aquellas bacantes que la sierra dio....* He looks for Silenus, who should preside over a Bacchanal; for the girls, in their excitement, look like Bacchantes (since, bearing no quiver, they cannot be huntress-nymphs).

275–80. 'Or—if the stream tumbling from the craggy mountains can be thought to resemble the Thermodon—the girls may be an unarmed troop of Amazons waving peaceful banners.'

281. *lascivo:* 'playful' here.

282–3. 'Unimpeded by the yoke of marriage [i.e. all gay bachelors], in the judgement of the youth [*al voto del mancebo*].'

284–6. I.e. *impedido de flores* (wreathed in flowers) *el rayo nuevo* (the calf's budding horn) *que ya serenaba la región de su frente* (made serene its forehead as the sun's rays make serene the heavens).

289. *entre albogues se ofrece:* 'appears to the sound of pipes'.

291–2. 'One of them descends bearing hanging from his hands heavy bundles of black, crested hens.'

294. I.e. *es doméstico nuncio canoro del Sol:* '(the cock) the barnyard herald of the sun'.

295–6. 'Bearded with coral, he wears not a golden but a crimson turban (his comb).'

297–302. 'Another carries slung round his neck some speckled kids, the most playful of the flock, so greedy that the one who cannot reach (with his teeth) the flowers adorning him complains.'

303–5. 'The timid rabbit's peace was not preserved by its craggy home or twisting burrows in the mountains.'

308. *si...no:* once again this expresses equivalence: 'and a heavy load and source of wonder (by their number)'.

309. The turkey.

312–14. Salcedo Coronel explained: 'El pavo no tiene cresta, sino cierta piel carnosa y colorada; la qual estiende de suerte que cubre el rostro, principalmente quando está enojado...': 'let the turkey be ever so angry, it is still destined for the wedding-feast'.

315–20. 'On a pole supported by two shoulders are seen a hundred ruby beaks on a hundred birds (partridges), shod with finest crimson leather, vying with—or even outshining—amidst those rude crags the craftsmanship of the Berbers.'

321–6. 'The tears of Dawn—if she weeps nectar—drunk, before the sun is up to dry them, by the bee, early abroad to sip the flowers and the crystalline dew': i.e. the dew which Góngora supposes to go to make the honey carried in the earthen pots by the *montañés* of 328.

329–34. 'The fawn, whose horn (*el pululante ramo*) is no longer than his ear, struggles as he is led, and rightly: for even the shadow of a horn, however small, is repugnant to the marriage-bed' (since horns symbolise cuckoldry).

335–9. Instead of following the roundabout road, the *serranas* have taken a short cut, which is like a string to the road's bow. The heavily burdened youths went by the road.

340–1. The bearers set their loads down for a rest, as if making a truce with their burdens.

344–9. 'Thanks to the beauty it has entertained (a reference to 240–58), unless it was the sweet effect which the harmonious rhythm of the black stones (slates?: the clappers of 251)—like stony strings strung on shining ivory pegs (the fingers of the *serrana*)—had on the stream's headlong course, so long as the wind withheld its fury.'

354–5. 'Resting their cares of love on the red roses worn by the maids': presumably the young men rest their heads in the laps of the *serranas*, who wear red skirts. Or perhaps the roses are on the maidens' bosoms.

363. I.e. *las cerúleas señas*...: the sea-water stains.

366–71. I.e. *Cuál tigre, la más fiera que infamó clima hircano, dio*...*al labrador fiero que primero surcó el campo undoso, ya deste o* [*de*] *aquel mar, en mal nacido pino*....

372–3. Clytie, who loved Apollo, was turned into the sunflower, which keeps its face always turned to the sun. As Clytie is to the sun, sails ('flax turned into sailcloth not a flower') are to the wind.

374–8. The invention of the ship has brought more strife to shores divided by the sea than the Trojan horse introduced into Troy.

379–92. The loadstone—of which the compass-needle was made—clings to iron (*el metal fulminante de que Marte se viste*) more closely than ivy to a rock. It seeks out the Polestar (*el diamante que más brilla*, etc.). The star, when far off (when the compass is not far north), attracts the needle; but when the star is overhead the needle swings restlessly between east (*al rosado balcón de la Aurora bella*) and west (*la cerúlea tumba fría que sella las cenizas al día*)—the effect of proximity to Magnetic North.

393–5. I.e. *fiándose en esta atractiva amante dura del Norte* (the loadstone) *no hay tormentoso cabo que no doble el alado roble* (the ship)....

397–402. Tiphys: the pilot of the Argo; Palinurus: Aeneas' helmsman. 'These sailed only one sea (the Mediterranean), which the earth made into a lake, the Strait (of Gibraltar) being locked by the Pillars of Hercules as if by keys.'

403–10. I.e. *la Codicia*...*dejó al padre de las aguas, Océano*...*cano de su espuma*.

411–12. 'Greed admits no rival in sailing to the uttermost parts of the earth.'

413–18. 'Greed sent three ships (of Columbus) to steal from Neptune a part of his domains hitherto unexplored (*violaron aquel tridente a Neptuno*), reaching the blue curtains that the West draws on the sun when he sinks to sleep in his bed of blue water.'

419. *áspides volantes:* poisoned arrows, which seem to infect the very air (*tósigo del viento*).

421. *sus banderas*, etc.: the banners of Greed, to which Góngora attributes the feats of the *Conquistadores*.

423–4. I.e. *los lestrigones* (*aladas fieras*) *que el istmo armó de cien plumas.* Góngora transfers the name of Laestrygones—mythical cannibals supposed to inhabit Sicily and Campania—to the Caribs, armed with deadly arrows flighted with feathers. The isthmus is that of Panama.

425–9. 'The isthmus that divides the Ocean, which coils round the earth like a crystal serpent, dividing its head, crowned with the North, from the scaly tail that the South lights with Antarctic stars': i.e. dividing Atlantic from Pacific (known as *Mar del Norte* and *Mar del Sur* respectively).

430–4. The next ocean to be explored was the Pacific (*segundo polo* refers to its name of *Mar del Sur*), 'which yielded not only pearls but the deadly metals that Midas found of little profit'. Midas' touch of gold deprived him of food and even of his child. Góngora here alludes to the strife and corruption attendant on gold and silver.

439–40. I.e. *tantas señas del....*

443–6. Greed has ferried many over the Styx (has caused many deaths) and is undeterred by the danger of a watery grave.

447–8. The normal construction would be: *El promontorio cuyas rocas hizo Éolo candados...*: an allusion to Aeolus' shutting up of the winds, which Góngora associates with the stormy Cape of Good Hope, first rounded by Vasco da Gama on his voyage to India in 1498.

453–6. I.e. [*Después de*] *frustados tantos...presagios* [*y*] *tanta náutica doctrina*, etc.

458–60. I.e. *cuyos purpúreos senos* [*te guardan*] *perlas netas*, *cuyas minas... te guardan su más precioso engaste:* pearls and the precious metals that will form a setting for them.

461. *aromática selva:* aromatic because of its frankincense, for which Arabia was famous.

462–4. The Phoenix, 'whose flight is like a winged rainbow—but straight, not curved'.

466–80. The circumnavigation of the world by one of Magellan's ships, the *Victoria*, is here described. (Magellan himself was killed during the voyage). The sea was a *cristalino zodíaco* for the *glorioso pino*—the *Victoria*—which, after sailing for 400 days (470–1), entered the Pacific through the Strait of Magellan (*la bisagra de fugitiva plata*) uniting the two oceans which are in reality one, 'whether it kiss the pillars (of Hercules) or Dawn's scarlet carpet': i.e. for Góngora the extremes of West and East.

481. I.e. *no te describo la inmóvil flota de firmes islas...*: the Spice Islands. See p. 27.

487. Diana and her huntresses, seen bathing in the river Eurotas by

Actaeon, who was as a punishment turned into a stag and was killed by his own dogs.

488. *pario:* Parian: marble from Paros was prized for its whiteness.

492. The clove.

496. A pun on *clavo*, 'clove' and 'nail': 'the clove, not a restraint but a spur to appetite'.

501. I.e. *la mejor prenda del alma:* his son.

502. A remote allusion to Prometheus, on whose liver an eagle was set by Zeus to feed for ever.

503–6. I.e. *anegó el resto de su discurso...en más suspiros* [*que los soplos con*] *que el viento anegó su caudal, en más lágrimas* [*que las olas con*] *que el mar anegó su hijo.*

518. *neutralidad:* 'lack of a fixed plan'.

522. *política:* 'courteous'—because of its shade.

534–9. I.e. *la* [*arboleda de la cual*]—*si no era calle de chopos*, etc.—*el fresco ruido...el denso celaje...ponen en duda cuál hacía mayor guerra... o mayor resistencia al día.* Though the grove is not a formal avenue of trees, it is pleasant for its coolness and shade.

540. *Coros tejiendo:* 'dancing'.

545–6. *pedazos de cristal:* glimpses of the white ankles of the *serranas*; *que el movimiento*, etc.: 'which their movements as they dance grant to their skirts and their skirts to their shoes': the swinging of their skirts allows a glimpse of bare legs between skirt and shoe.

547–9. A shoe is a 'jealous' base of the legs because it hides the foot, but at the same time is prodigal of the *cristal* because the dancing feet allow the girls' legs to be seen.

550. 'Seeming by their harmonious singing to be sirens of those hills.'

551–5. I.e. *el menor paso...hiciera dar pasos a la antigua planta que menos pudiera temer....*

559–60. The stream's purling over its pebbles gives it the appearance of having ears.

561. 'From its source to where it ends' (that is, in a river or the sea).

562–3. 'The *serranos*—already imagining themselves victorious—award themselves the prizes for the morrow's sports.'

566–7. I.e. *el menos ágil, él solo desafía cuantos comarcanos el caso convoca.*

568. *palios:* the palio was a silk cloth awarded as a prize.

569–72. 'Who dries with many a rose-petal the sweat of his brow, greater already than the sweat he expects the morrow's sports to produce.'

573–5. I.e. *un círculo espacioso, bien de pobos, bien de alisos, hacía* [*un*] *centro....*

577. Greek accusatives: 'shod with...clothed in...'.

578–80. 'Spring makes a stream flow from a crag ringed with daffodils, as if it struck watery sparks from a flint.'

580. I.e. *Este centro era, pues, meta....*

585–6. The girls stop to drink from the murmuring stream.

588–9. I.e. *y cela la verde tela...:* 'and hides the net laid for them'.

591. *verdes canas:* the poplar's leaves, green above, white below.

594. The *montañés* may be the old man, in his grief insensible to the beauties of Nature; or the word may be a collective term for all the *montañeses* of the party, in too great a hurry to enjoy what they see and hear.

598–600. I.e. *atribuye aún mayor veneno a cuantas sierpes de aljófar da la fuente que a las del Ponto:* 'seems to believe the streams gushing from the spring to be more bitter than sea-water'.

601. 'To judge by the way he hurries away without drinking.' *Huir* is here used transitively.

602. *regulados:* 'drawn up in order'.

609. I.e. *formando caracteres alados:* 'forming winged letters'.

613. *pintadas...al fresco:* a punning allusion to fresco painting; these leafy vaults are always 'painted' (bright with colour) and 'al fresco' (in cool shade).

614–15. I.e. [*las serranas*] *cubren las verdes alfombras que....* Here *sidón* must be an adjective; it alludes to Turkish carpet-weaving in Syria, near the site of ancient Sidon.

621–2. *de presentes prevenidas:* 'prepared with gifts'.

626–9. I.e. *la sombra florida vio cuajada nieve* (the snowy limbs of the girls, gaily clothed), etc.

630–2. I.e. *que a ellas igualmente les quedaba de camino...:* they were as close to the village as the sun was to setting.

640–1. The smoking chimneys of the village are 'watchtowers of the West' in that they announce the approach of sunset.

645–6. They arrive when daylight has given way to the light of the rockets (*errante fuego*) fired from the church tower (*sacro volcán*).

649–50. I.e. *da saetas luminosas de pólvora exhalada.*

651. The rockets are signs of rejoicing, not ill-omen, as comets would be.

652. *solemniza:* 'praises'.

653–5. The old man is disturbed lest one of the lights bring by night the disaster that Phaeton brought by day: that is, set fire to the place.

659–62. I.e. *las plantas de Alcides:* poplars, into which the sisters of Phaeton were turned, and sacred to Hercules. They plait their hair by the light of the fires, using the stream as a mirror.

665–8. 'The sun would gladly shrink into a star (in order to witness this night scene) the rays that the Bengalese—dark swan of Ganges—greets (at dawn).'

671–2. At the sound the most fixed star moves and trees dance. The Triones are the seven stars of the Plough.

673–6. Every momentary silence is filled by an echo (of the gaiety)—and by a loud echo (not the usual faint sound).

679. *prolijo:* a favourite adjective of Góngora's: here 'lasting' (because the effects of the dancing are slow to wear off).

690–4. I.e. *el golpe...deja desnudo al verde aliso de su esplendor, de su frondosa pompa.*

699. Because the lovers' names carved on it will now be read.

707–8. An allusion to the first light of dawn.

718–19. I.e. *y los arcos* [*de rosas*] *que fabrican.*

720. 'New, oblique hanging gardens' (like those of Babylon). Oblique because of the shape of the arches.

727–31. 'Just as the openings of the green bud in which the unopened rose compresses its beauty are fringed with a hue that the crimson hidden within allows timidly to be glimpsed.'

732–6. The subject is *el joven,* suddenly reminded of her who scorned him.

737–42. 'His mistress' sun burns to ashes the black plumes of mourning that clothe his memory, but they beget a silent worm (of despair) whose tooth, which once slowly sapped his joy, now undyingly turns up furrows from which springs his grief.'

743–9. The *labradora*'s complexion is compounded of lily and carnation, and its beauty tries to emulate the more tempered beauty of his mistress. 'In the shadow of the lily...the youth's thoughts tread on a snake (of grief) so poisonous that his soul—poured forth in tears through his eyes—would have given clear signs of his transport' (if he were not again distracted by the new arrivals).

755–7. I.e. *al fin el numeroso concurso...saca....*

760. As if she were the sphere itself that (in Ptolemy's system) contains the sun.

761–3. 'Hymen (god of marriage) was wreathing their necks in the bonds of marriage, amidst a playful swarm of amoretti.'

764–5. I.e. *la alterna voz tierna....*

768. 'A youth as amorous as Cupid, but a real man, so without wings and not blindfold.'

769–70. 'His boyishly long hair belies the down that covers his face.'

772. His hair is golden, like the sun.

773. As a child he loved her whom now he adores as a youth.

775–6. I.e. *en los inciertos crepúsculos...:* between girl and woman. She is the object of *vincule.*

781. *previene:* 'forestalls': she is like a dawn before the real dawn.

784. *dos soles:* her eyes.

786–91. I.e. *Cuantos claveles...engasta el oro del cabello, cuantas rosas la concordia ya engarza* [*en*] *cadenas del uno y del otro cuello, son purpúreos trofeos de sus mejillas...:* carnations and roses pale by comparison with her blushing cheeks.

793–4. I.e. *los hijuelos alados de las bellas ninfas...den plumas...:* 'let the amoretti—children of the nymphs—take to the air...'.

799–800. I.e. *del pájaro nocturno que más tardo vuela o* [*más*] *triste gime.*

803–4. The metaphor describes the love-making of groom and bride. Hybla in Sicily was famous for its honey.

806. *volantes pías:* the peacocks of Juno, protectress of women: *pías* because like piebald horses they draw her chariot.

807–8. *que...sus plumas = cuyas plumas.*

810. *fíe:* 'stand surety for'.

813–14. *Lucina:* a name of Juno when she presides over birth. 'Let Lucina cross her threshold so often in different months' (let the bride bear many children).

815–17. Niobe had many children but she was punished by the gods for her presumptuous boasting: she was turned into marble, which Góngora makes a rock of Lethe, the river of forgetfulness. 'Let the world admire her as a new Niobe, but not as marble....'

819–21. I.e. *nuestra agricultura deba a estrellas amigas progenie tan robusta, de tal copia que....*

824–6. I.e. *blancas ovejas suyas hagan caducar la hierba al verde...llano.*

827. The *oro líquido* is olive oil, from the tree of Minerva.

829–30. Vines, sacred to Lyaeus (Bacchus), were trained to grow up elms, from whose wood the club of Hercules was made. Hence, grapes seem to crown Hercules, while Bacchus grasps Hercules' club (as his tendrils cling to the elms).

832–3. Pales was god (or goddess) of flocks and herds, Pallas the patroness of weaving. Hence: 'may she have as many boys as girls'.

838–41. 'Let not the girls, as skilled in weaving as Arachne but more modest, portray the rapes and amorous wiles of Jupiter.'

842–3. Both allusions are to Jupiter, who enjoyed Danae by taking the form of a golden shower and Leda by taking that of a swan.

846. *revocó:* 'accompanied back'.

848–51. 'The newly married couple returns home, as young oxen, scarcely broken to the yoke, return after only a little ploughing to their thatched byre, the plough hanging between them.'

857. *previno:* 'prepared'.

858–60. I.e. *artífice gentil...ostente crespas blancas esculturas en los manteles que Flandes damascó:* 'let serving-men at court, skilled in folding linen, set out damask cloths of Flanders that resemble white sculpture'.

861–4. 'While home-woven linen here displays the fruits of Ceres—all the apples that were kept in hay to ripen, so ripe and golden that Atalanta would have stopped for them.' (Hippomenes beat her in a race by throwing golden apples that she stopped to pick up.)

867–71. I.e. *confuso Baco no les desata su néctar en oro luciente...sino en...:* Bacchus is confused because many wines are mingled, so that the topaz-coloured (yellow) become red, and the red pale.

872–5. I.e. *rubio quesillo...quiso sellar los gulosos estómagos del fuego:* the cheese tried to temper the fire of the wine.

881–2. An allusion to the popular belief that the olive prevents drunkenness. The metaphor recalls the olive-branch that was a sign of the abatement of the Flood.

883–4. To the sound of the pipes, made of the reeds into which Syrinx was changed.

886–7. *el sutil oro*, etc.: 'their golden hair which well-woven ribbons—the colour of mother-of-pearl—restrained from flying in the wind'.

888–9. That is, they form groups of three.

897–900. 'May the thread of life that Clotho transfers from distaff to bobbin (i.e. spins) be whiter than snow and in its whiteness look like carded silver.' That is, may their life know only the colour of joy.

901–3. 'May your efforts be rewarded by the applause of Fortune.'

904–8. I.e. [*que*] *el campo fecundo—agradecido a la reja importuna—os rinda oro trillado....*

909–12. That is, may their goats and cattle be more numerous than the trees on the mountainside.

914–16. *que...su número = cuyo número.*

917–18. I.e. *cuantos vellones la tijera les desnuda.*

922. I.e. *cual la Arabia, madre de aromas, ve....*

929. The asp was associated with envy; *la región del llanto:* Hell.

930–3. 'May time—following a middle course between opulence and poverty—bestow a middling competence on your children, avoiding both extremes.'

939. 'When the head of each is white as the plumage of the swan....'

942–3. 'May your tombstone be inscribed with lessons of disillusion whose few words long ages will read.'

949. A Greek accusative: 'dressed in...'.

953. The Nile.

955. I.e. *no pequeños vacíos:* Góngora believed that the Pyramids had disappeared, leaving empty spaces behind.

958–60. The foliage that had earlier formed an artificial bower is now withdrawn to leave the village green clear.

966–7. *menos defendidos*, etc.: 'less covered with linen than with hair'.

971. *implicantes vides:* 'enfolding vines'—trained to grow up the elms.

973. The allusion is to Antaeus, son of Earth, with whom Hercules (Alcides) wrestled.

983. *expedido:* 'light-footed'.

984. *la bárbara corona:* 'the surrounding rustic multitude'.

987. *a quien se abaten:* 'for which [eight or ten lads from the hills] come down into the arena'.

988–91. 'As a flock of birds will often swoop to mob the lazy-winged owl, as if envious of its golden eyes.' Ascalaphus was turned into an owl for betraying Persephone.

993. *pondera:* 'boasts of'.

995. *la raya:* the starting-line.

996. *suelto:* 'fleet'.

997–8. 'Jumped three javelin-lengths of the village green': *pisó del viento* pictures him as treading the wind.

999. A synecdoche: *admiración* means the admiring (or astonished) onlookers, seemingly turned into marble.

1001. *la emulación:* 'those who would emulate the leap'—seemingly rooted, their feet as if in shackles of ice.

1007–9. *violentando*, etc.: 'doing such violence to gravity that his own weight brings him down, like an Icarus of the mountains' (so that he falls on grass, not—like Icarus—into the sea).

1010–11. I.e. *el seno blando de la menuda hierba hecho piélago duro*....

1016–17. The moufflon. Góngora may be using *trepar* in the very unusual sense of 'to climb down' (instead of the normal 'climb *up*'); or he may be using it in an older sense, 'to tumble head over heels', in allusion to a belief that the moufflon when alarmed threw itself down headlong from the rocks, landing on its unusually hard head (and hence leaving no footmark). See J. Arce, 'El muflón sardo en unos versos de Góngora...', *Revista de filología española*, LXV (1964), 1–19.

1023. 'Yet another leapt, treading the air and kicking the ground.'

1024. *graduadamente:* 'according to their deserts'.

1039. *o nervïosos*, etc.: 'strong either with sinew or with steel'.

1041–2. 'They raise no dust to obscure the countryside, for they seem to fly and not to tread the grass.'

1052. *la distancia sincopan:* 'shrink the distance'—by their speed.

1054–7. I.e. *no abrazó Apolo más firme, más estrechamente los dulces... miembros de la Peneida virgen* [Daphne] *en la corteza reciente* ('newly turned into a laurel and covered with bark').

1061–2. 'I doubt if Alcides himself—to whom the elms are sacred—could decide which was the winner.'

1065. 'While the token of victory remains unawarded.'

1070–2. 'Anticipates the beams of the planet Venus which, blue at evening, red at dawn, marks the twilit limits of the day.'

1073–6. The *padrino* of the wedding settles the question of who won the race by awarding three steel knives.

1081–3. 'Which is lit by fixed stars (torches) and by shooting stars (rockets) which explode amidst a cloud of smoke.'

1086–7. The allusion is to the doves that draw Venus' chariot.

1088. *entra:* transitive here: 'ushers in'.

## II 'FÁBULA DE POLIFEMO Y GALATEA'

2. *Talía:* Thalia, Muse first of lyric and pastoral poetry (hence *bucólica*), later of comedy.

5. *Niebla:* the seat of the Conde de Niebla (to whom the poem is dedicated), now adorned with his presence.

9–10. 'Let the falcon, now at rest on the falconer's hand, preen its feathers.'

11–12. 'So silent...as to try (but in vain) to make it seem that it wears no bell.' Góngora urges the Count to leave the hunt to listen to his poetry.

20. *músico jayán:* Polyphemus.

26. *argenta de plata:* not a tautology: the verb ('to plate') had lost its association with silver.

26–31. *Lilibeo:* Lilybaeum, a promontory in south-west Sicily. According to myth, Typhoeus—one of the giants who rebelled against Jupiter and was killed—was buried under Etna (at the other end of the island), beneath which, according to another myth, lay Vulcan's forge. For Góngora, Lilybaeum is a conveniently poetic name which can be taken to stand for all Sicily.

32. The sense is: *sirve de mordaza de la boca de una gruta.*

37–9. I.e. *infame turba...nos enseña* [*que*] *el seno obscuro* [*es*] *caliginoso lecho de la negra noche.*

46–7. I.e. *cuanto cabrío esconde las cumbres ásperas...:* Polyphemus' goats cover the mountainside.

47. *copia:* 'abundance': Polyphemus' goats.

48. 'Which Polyphemus summons with a whistle and shuts in (in the cave) with a rock.'

49. *eminente:* 'towering'—a Latinism.

52. His single eye is almost as large as the sun.

53–4. 'Whom the stoutest pine served as a stick.'

56. That is, it bent beneath his weight.

59–60. I.e. *vuela al viento...sin orden....*

62. *adusto:* 'rough' or 'shaggy' here.

65–8. 'Trinacria (Sicily) has not bred in its mountains a beast endowed with savagery or speed enough to save its skin marked with a hundred hues': that is, from Polyphemus, who now wears the skins of fierce animals he has slain.

69. *la* [*fiera*].

71. *reducía:* 'led back'.

73. 'Polyphemus' bag, as full as it is capacious, encloses the fruit—now almost bursting from it (*abortado*)—which tardy Autumn entrusts to the soft bosom of the compassionate grass' (the fruit being put in hay to ripen).

79–80. *pálida tutora*, etc.: the hay hides the pear—as a guardian should—while assiduously covering it with gold as it ripens (as a guardian increases his ward's estate).

81. *Erizo:* the word can mean the prickly husk of chestnuts, etc. Polyphemus' *zurrón* is like a protective *erizo* for the fruits it contains.

83–4. The apple's ruddy skin hides its white interior—unlike the hypocrite, whose candid and innocent exterior hides other hues within.

85–8. I.e. *y el tributo de la encina* (*honor...*), *alimento...del mejor mundo, del candor primero:* that is, the acorn, food of the fabled Golden Age. The construction of the whole stanza offers difficulties. The best solution appears to be: *Erizo es el zurrón de la castaña y...de la manzana ...y* [*de*] *el tributo de la encina....*

89–90. Polyphemus' pan-pipes.

97–8. I.e. *adora* [*una*] *ninfa, hija de Doris....*

100. 'Venus sums up in her the beauty of her three Graces' (*terno:* 'trio').

101–2. Galatea's skin suggests the whiteness of the swan. Her eyes suggest the 'eyes' on a peacock's tail. Hence she unites the beauty of swan and peacock.

104. The swan is the bird of Venus, the peacock of Juno. Their attributes are mingled in Galatea.

109–10. I.e. *la perla eritrea es émula vana de su frente:* it cannot compete with her in whiteness.

110–12. Cupid, angered by the pearl's presumption, condemns it to hang—from Galatea's ear (as an earring).

113–14. I.e. *era...cuidado de cuantas deidades el mar honra:* the sea-gods are in love with her.

116. Cupid, being blindfold, steers blindly (without a lantern) the shell that is one of the symbols of Venus.

118–20. The shore hears the voice of Glaucus trying to persuade Galatea to course the ocean in his crystal chariot.

124. 'From the lighthouse of Messina (hateful for the danger of

that coast) to the promontory of Lilybaeum.' (I follow Pellicer in this.)

125–6. Palaemon receives no more favour than Polyphemus from Galatea, though her scorn is somewhat less.

127. *calzada plumas:* a Greek accusative: 'with winged feet'.

132. Palaemon would like to be a golden apple, to stay Galatea's flight as Atalanta's was stayed.

137–8. Sicily is like the goblet of Bacchus in her abundance of wine (hidden in wine-cellars) and in her abundance of fruits like the orchard of Pomona.

142. *perdona:* 'spare': Ceres makes Sicily yield continuously.

145–6. 'The verdant hills owe to Pales (goddess of flocks) as much as, or more than, the plains to Ceres': the island is as abundant in sheep as in grain.

148. I.e. *en la otra nieva mil copos de lana.*

149–50. *oro...nieve...grana:* grain, wool and wine.

153–6. I.e. ...*que el margen del espumoso mar donde para* [*Galatea*] *su pie ligero es al labrador* [*un*] *ara de sus primicias, y al ganadero* [*ara*] *de sus esquilmos.*

157–8. The *hortelano* pours out (into the wicker baskets of line 159) the Horn of Plenty, which gives generously to the earth (of Sicily).

165–7. I.e. ...*los ganados ignoran los crujidos resonantes de las hondas* (the slings with which the Mediterranean shepherd controls his flock).

169–70. 'Silent by night, asleep by day, the dog just sleeps around from hill to hill and shade to shade': he is as neglectful of his duty as his master.

175. *Revoca:* 'bring back'—'make the shepherd attend to his flock again'.

175–6. *o a su dueño*, etc.: 'or let the silent and sleeping (hence useless) dog follow his master'.

178–80. Galatea bathes, giving to the spring as many jasmines (her white skin) as the grass which her snowy-white body hides as she lies down at the water's edge.

184. *tres soles:* her eyes as well as the real sun.

185–6. The sun enters the constellation of the Dog (Canis major) at the height of summer. The Dog seems to bark (give out yet more heat) and, because of the sun's heat, resembles the salamander, able to live in fire. These are in fact the dog-days.

187–8. *húmidas centellas*, etc.: Acis is so hot that his sweat suggests watery sparks or burning pearls.

189–90. 'Seeing the beautiful eyes of Galatea hidden in sleep as the sun is hidden at sunset....'

191–2. I.e. *dio su boca al sonoro cristal* (the water that he drinks) *y sus ojos cuanto pudo al cristal mudo* (the white form of Galatea).

193. Acis was as straight as a lance, and an appropriate weapon for Cupid to wound hearts with.

195. *habido:* 'begotten'.

197–8. Acis is the subject of both verbs: 'The beautiful loadstone (Galatea), the sleeping idol, to whom he is drawn like steel, he idolatrously adores....'

200. *fomenta el robre:* probably honey is referred to, not acorns.

201–2. Though there is some ambiguity, Góngora probably referred to shelled (but not dried) almonds here.

208. *vinculó:* 'joined'.

212. 'Stand like two green herons in the stream.'

213–16. 'The breeze blows gently (round the sleeping Galatea) as if drawing imaginary curtains round her bed, made not of air but of shade and fine greensward.'

217–18. I.e. *Apenas sintió la ninfa bullir la sonorosa plata del arroyuelo.*

220. *segur:* some early versions had *seguir*, but *segur* is preferred by the best modern editors on stylistic grounds. The image (a difficult one) seems to describe Galatea springing up in alarm, separating her white body from the grass on which she had lain, as lilies are mown by a sickle.

223. *precisa:* necessary, that is, in Galatea's eyes.

227–8. Probably: *si bien su deidad culta debe, agradecida, el sueño venerado al dueño:* 'her adored deity gratefully owes to their (the gifts') owner the fact that she was worshipped while asleep'.

229. *A la ausencia...ofrecida:* 'disposed to flee'.

230–1. I.e. *este no pequeño indicio de cortesía....*

232. *más discursiva:* 'more affable'.

235–6. 'Whose self-restraint, relaxed by desire, may dreams strain further' (by offering illusory temptations).

247–8. Galatea 'regrets that the devoted [and devout, since he worships her] owner of the gift-offering should be hidden a moment longer [*más*] by the green grove which, densely concealing [*confuso*], is like a warder of the one it hides'.

258. 'Balancing on one foot, she leans over him.'

259. *urbana...bárbara:* the sense is complex. Galatea is 'courteous' to Acis' feigned sleep in that she tries not to disturb it. But *bárbara* is used in its original sense: 'foreign', 'strange', hence 'uncomprehending' (since Galatea does not see through Acis' silent stratagem). *Urbana*, as its opposite, then comes to mean also 'familiar with', 'comprehending'.

261. *ave reina:* the eagle.

275. *admira:* 'astonish' here.

277–8. Acis' hair emulates the colour of the sun's rays at sunset.

280. Since Acis' eyes are closed (and so their brightness hidden), the colour of the down on his face cannot easily be seen.

285. *vulto:* 'face'.

289–90. *aún más*, etc.: 'even more watchful of what the peephole of sleep (his half-open eyelids) allows him to see...' (that is, Galatea's expression).

295–6. *paladïones:* a reference to the Palladium, which was the statue of Pallas on whose preservation the safety of Troy depended. Góngora, alluding to the fall of Troy, means here: 'for into her innermost sanctuaries blind Cupid carries the fire of love, but without the need to overthrow walls'.

315–16. That is, Spring—silkworm and weaver in one—spun and wove her carpet of flowers.

317. *reclinados:* 'while the lovers recline' (two doves perch on the myrtle).

320. The amorous cooing of the doves is like a summons to love's war (because the sound suggests the rolling of drums).

323–4. Since *plaudere* in Latin could mean 'caress', Dámaso Alonso suggests (*Góngora y el 'Polifemo'*, II, 208) that the lines may mean: 'Galatea sets bounds to Acis' audacity and to the lovers' caresses, limiting caresses to the intermingling harmony of the birds.' A simpler interpretation might be: 'Setting bounds to Acis' audacity and limiting the birds' harmonious applause' (since they seem to applaud the scene of love).

325–8. The allusion is to Tantalus, condemned to perpetual thirst though with water and fruit apparently within his reach. *Fugitivo cristal* is Galatea's elusive form, *pomos de nieve* her white breasts.

329. *No:* this has the force of *apenas* here.

331–2. Acis kisses Galatea.

339. *las columnas...que erigió el griego:* the pillars of Hercules: i.e. the west. *Etón:* Aethon, one of the horses of Phoebus' chariot.

344. The rock is a warning to ships: hence a 'lightless lighthouse'.

345. *Árbitro:* because he stands between them dominating both.

351. Galatea is clinging passionately to Acis.

360. *Pïérides:* the Muses.

372. *en dos* [*soles*].

375. An allusion to a traditional belief concerning the origin of pearls.

380. That is, when Galatea retires to sleep beneath the sea.

387. *desparezco:* transitive here: 'I make disappear.'

395. *corchos:* hives of cork. The construction is: *más corchos que* [*las*] *flores que* [*la*] *abeja liba....*

401. Neptune was his father.

406. *tanto esposo:* 'so great a husband'.

413. *¿Qué mucho...?:* 'And is that surprising...?'

417–18. 'The halcyon sat on its eggs above a towering crag....' That is, Polyphemus saw his reflection in the calm sea of a halcyon day.

421–4. Polyphemus' eye rivals the sun's size, so that the sea is unable to decide which is which.

425–6. 'The stag's head hangs over other doors, revealing its age' (indicated by its antlers).

427–8. '...the boar, whose bristling back is like a wall of sharp Swiss pikes.'

435–6. I.e. *grave de cuantas riquezas vomitó el Orïente por las bocas del Nilo.*

437–40. Polyphemus' pipes soothed the waves that day.

443. *aromas del Sabeo:* Saba, in Arabia, was famous for its frankincense and myrrh.

454. Two ways of ripening and keeping fruit.

455–6. The elephant.

461–2. Polyphemus offers bow and quiver to Galatea who, already more beautiful than Venus, can then imitate Cupid, her son (who carries a bow). *Convencida* probably retains its Latin sense, 'overcome'.

468. 'Attacked the plants of Bacchus'—vines.

469–70. I.e. *viendo el fiero pastor el pámpano...conculcado.*

470–1. 'He uttered so many shouts and discharged so many stones from his sling.'

472. *el muro...:* behind which Acis and Galatea shelter.

478. *meseguero:* one who guards the crops.

479. I.e. *así dirimió* [*una*] *copia amiga de liebres. copia:* 'couple' here (an Italianism); *dirimió:* 'separated'.

482. *la fugitiva nieve:* the white, fleeing form of Galatea.

483–4. 'For to eyes as keen as those of Polyphemus the small compass of the Libyan's shield is clearly displayed.' Polyphemus can see from Sicily to Africa. *Registrar* here means 'show', 'display'.

492. *urna:* 'a funerary urn'.

495–6. The sense is: *la sangre que exprimió el peñasco duro, cristal fue puro.*

## III SONNETS

### 1

9–14. Góngora urges the stream to carry his mistress's reflection carefully to the sea so as not to spoil the image of her beauty.

### 3

4. *el garzón de Ida:* Ganymede.

## 4

9–10. The sonnet was written during a stay in Granada. The sestet is a clear reminiscence of Psalm 137: 'If I forget thee, O Jerusalem, let my right hand forget its cunning. If I do not remember thee, let my tongue cleave to the roof of my mouth; if I prefer not Jerusalem above my chief joy.'

## 5

This sonnet probably reflects a real experience. Góngora fell seriously ill in Salamanca in 1593 and may, during his convalescence, have fallen in love as the sonnet recounts (see Artigas, pp. 71–3). But it has also been pointed out that the sonnet is in the *serranilla* tradition, then enjoying a revival. See B. W. Wardropper, 'Góngora and the *serranilla*', *Modern Language Notes* (1962), pp. 178–81.

## 6

Philip III's Queen, Margaret of Austria, died in 1611.

6. An allusion to the candles on the *túmulo*, resembling St Elmo's fire, taken by sailors to be a sign of divine protection.

7–8. The sense is: *serenan la volubilidad reconocida de la Fortuna.*

12. *Margarita:* a pun: the name means 'pearl'.

## 7

1–2. I.e. *Esta dura llave* (the painter's tomb) *en forma elegante de pórfido luciente....*

3. 'Withholds from the world the most delicate brush....'

9–11. 'Nature inherits the body of the painter; his fellow-artists inherit his art to study; the rainbow inherits the colours of his palette; Phoebus, the brilliant light of his paintings; Morpheus, their shadows.'

12–14. 'May this tomb evoke tears...and all the balsams exuded by the funereal Sabaean tree.' 'Funereal' because of the solemn associations of incense, for which Saba was famous.

## 8

1. *occidental:* 'declining'.

6. The image is of a crumbling building.

7–8. 'What prudent man, warned by the falling dust, lingers to see the collapse of the whole building?'

9–10. An allusion to the belief that the snake is rejuvenated by sloughing its skin.

12–13. *la ponderosa porción:* the body. *una piedra muda:* a tombstone.

14. *la leve* [*porción*]*:* the soul.

## 9

3. *agonal:* agonistic (said of games in honour of Janus). *carro:* chariot.

8. *sol...cometa:* every sun that dawns becomes a sign of ill-omen, like a comet, because it warns of the approach of death.

13. *limando:* 'wearing away'.

## 10

1. *capilla:* an allusion both to Góngora's post of royal chaplain and to the chapel in which a condemned man spent his last night. Góngora's hopes had come to nothing; he was deeply in debt and despair, and already planning to leave the Court for Córdoba.

4. He is routed by hunger, like a besieged man.

5. To make this line scan, a strong caesura is necessary between *duda* and *es*.

6. I.e. *mayor* [*culpa*] *ser de condición encogida* ('reticent').

9–11. He feels as if on the eve of execution, so strait is his plight, but he still hopes for favour.

## 11

5–6. *Carmen* ('song', 'poem' in Latin) alludes to Góngora's career as a poet—considered, he suggests, too frivolous in a royal chaplain; *hábito* alludes to the habit of the Order of Santiago that he obtained for a nephew in 1622. *Hábito* converts *Carmen* into a punning allusion to the Carmelite Order. The sense is: 'If it was a sin to devote myself to poetry, the penitential habit I was once given is superfluous'—because Góngora had already earned only poverty and neglect at the end of his life. *Merced* in line 1 can now be seen as an allusion to the Order of Mercedarians and *compañía* in line 3 to the Jesuits (*Compañía de Jesús*).

8. *descalzo:* a reference to the poverty in which Góngora left Madrid and also a punning allusion to the discalced Carmelites.

9–10. 'The least subject—though an unworthy chaplain—of the greatest king....' But *mínimo* is also a punning allusion to 'Minim', a mendicant friar of the Order of St Francis of Paula. Góngora, through these jokes, is emphasising his present involuntary poverty and abstinence.

13–14. The allusion to poverty and abstinence is continued: his *cuadragesimal voto* (Lenten vow) is his enforced resolution to return to Córdoba in poverty, as if leaving the Court for provincial life were analogous to Christ's forty days in the wilderness. The *corrector santo* to whom he has vowed this penance is, presumably, his God; *corrector*, however, continues the allusion in lines 9–10 since the word means a superior of the Order of Minims.

The whole sonnet, beneath its apparent humour, is a poignant expression of Góngora's wretched situation in his last years.

# IV ROMANCES

## 2

15–16. Harpies, half women, half birds of prey, used to snatch away food and defile what they left with their excrement.

24. 'When they sound the *toque del alba*' (the summons to prayer at dawn).

30. *mayores de la marca:* the phrase means 'of outstanding beauty', but there is a pun on *mayor*, 'elderly'.

60. Opportunity was traditionally represented as having a lock of hair before but with the back of the head bald.

## 3

5. *Dragut:* a sixteenth-century Turkish pirate.
6. 'While his galley stood off Marbella' (near Málaga).
24. Because of her tears, more precious than pearls.
38. Christian galleys of the Knights of St John of Malta.

## 4

20. *descuento:* 'depreciation'.
23. The metaphor is taken from the Roman triumph. The captives pulling the chariot of *desengaño* will be *locas esperanzas*, etc.
40. *sabeo:* from Saba, famous for frankincense and myrrh.
55. *hacer auto:* make public penance for.
63. *argentó de plata:* see *Polifemo*, 26.
83–4. An allusion to the famous 'penance' performed by Amadis of Gaul under the name of Beltenebros in the Peña Pobre.
107–8. She is now only a source of discomfort to him.
109–110. He is full of what he cannot digest: his years of folly.

## 5

Calderón quotes this romance at length in his play *El príncipe constante*.

2. *cenetes:* a Berber tribe: the Zeneta.
41. *los Gelves:* Jerba was lost by the Spaniards in 1560.
50. *muriese:* i.e. of love and despair.

## 6

45–52. These two stanzas are not by Góngora (according to the Chacón manuscript) but they are necessary to complete the sense.

## 7

This romance on Hero and Leander begins *in medias res*. In 1610 Góngora wrote another designed to precede it.

1. *mancebito:* Leander. Góngora begins his deflation of the story in the first line.

6. *pedorreras:* a variety of close-fitting breeches.

7. *Abido:* Abydos.

11. *candil:* the lamp lit by Hero to guide Leander.

15. *se desatacó:* 'unfastened its breeches'.

19–20. Aeolus entrusted the winds, shut up in a bag, to Ulysses, referred to as *el griego de los embustes* because of his wiliness. The episode is in *Odyssey* x.

22–3. Xerxes crossed the Hellespont on a bridge of boats.

31. *Sesto:* Hero was priestess of Aphrodite at Sestos.

48. *ubres:* a plebeian delicacy: another burlesque detail.

59. *palanquines vientos:* the winds toss him ashore like rough litter-bearers.

71–2. That is, Hell. *Pastillas* were burnt to perfume the air; these, however, are of brimstone.

82. The lovers are at last joined—but only by the epitaph scratched by Hero's maid with a bodkin drawn from her needlecase.

91–2. *pasado por agua:* Leander's fate was like that of an egg: the phrase means 'boiled'; *estrellada:* Hero was dashed to the ground and so her fate, too, resembles an egg's: *estrellada* means 'fried'.

## 9

The subject, the story of Angelica and Medoro, is taken from Ariosto (see p. 18).

9. Medoro, 'badly wounded but well attended' because Angelica is his nurse.

11–12. He enjoys the favours of love without its pains since Angelica fell in love with him first.

15–16. *aquella...:* Angelica, the life of men when she inspires them with hope, their death when she causes them to despair.

19–20. Medoro is surrounded with flowers, as if the grass repays by this means the blood he has shed.

23–4. The normal construction would be: *cuyos colores la muerte va violando.*

26–8. An allusion to an old belief that diamonds may be softened with blood. Angelica, princess of Cathay and hitherto hard-hearted though now moved to pity by Medoro's blood, is the diamond to be refashioned by Love's darts.

31–2. Because born amidst the pangs of love.

33–5. Angelica's heart, once hard as flint, is now struck by Love's arrow and she weeps for pity of Medoro. Since a flint gives out sparks when struck, her tears are *centellas*—but of water.

44. 'May the sun's beams spare her' (by not burning her unprotected face).

53–5. I.e. *la simple bondad, que mejor se halla....*

60. Because Medoro now possesses Angelica's heart, too.

67. Medoro, in whom Angelica's soul lives, as well as his own.

68. Angelica, blind with love, though her eyes are like two suns.

77–8. Angelica gives her beauty and her kingdom to Medoro, who thereby enjoys the first good fortune of Adonis, because Angelica is a Venus in beauty; and he becomes a second object of jealousy to Mars (who loved Venus), the first being Adonis. *Cuando menos* may mean that Angelica's beauty and kingdom are a less valuable dowry than her love.

85–8. One of Envy's attributes is the asp, in which she ties knots as she counts the amorous cooings of the two doves, Angelica and Medoro.

91. 'Lest she spread slanderous tales of the lovers.'

97–8. Because the cooing of the doves suggests the rolling of distant drums; but these are the drums of peace.

99. *volantes:* 'Género de adorno pendiente, que usaban las mujeres para la cabeza, hecho de tela delicada' (*Diccionario...de la Real Academia Española*). These are now Medoro's banners.

101. = *con el pecho desnudo:* a Greek accusative.

106. 'So that the snowy-whiteness of her skin may be set off.'

107–8. *no se vaya por pies:* a slang phrase: *irse por pies* is 'to take to one's heels'. The sense may then be: 'So that the beauty of the world (personified in Angelica) may not disappear'—because she is hobbled by the *lazos de oro*. This seems to be no more than a joke.

111–12. *lisonjeros...murmuradores:* the breezes are soothing (flattering) but without malice (*murmurar*, 'to backbite').

134. *contestes:* 'witnesses'.

136. An allusion to Count Orlando, approaching in hot pursuit.

## 10

1. *Júcar:* the river Júcar, in Cuenca, where Góngora went on behalf of his Chapter in 1603.

16. *no:* redundant to the sense: 'lest'. *mudanzas:* the word means 'a figure' (in dancing) but also 'change', 'fickleness'. The sense is: 'as they dance the girls hold hands in friendship, perhaps fearing it will be changed through fickleness, or the figures they dance'.

23–5. The girls wear blue *palmilla* (a cloth woven in Cuenca) which, though it is the colour of the heavens, is not the colour of hope but of jealousy.

28. *brújula:* 'peephole': the swinging of the skirts sometimes allows their feet to be glimpsed.

39. Her fingers.

49–52. Difficult lines. *Estar uno a partir un piñón con otro* is 'to be close friends with someone', *partir* here meaning 'to divide', 'share'. The verb also means 'to crack' (nuts—here pine-kernels). The sense of these lines may then be: 'Dancing together in close companionship —and cracking *piñones* in their pearly fingers....' (*Si no* evidently does not have here an antithetic sense: the girls are doing both.)

53–6. The girls are fancy-free: they gladly exchange the arrows of Love (to whom they are indifferent), some for *piñones*, some for dancing.

59–60. They tread on patches of sunlight (*ojos del sol*) filtering through the leaves; but the implication is also present that their eyes are brighter than the sun.

## 11

3. Blue is the colour of jealousy. Góngora is comforting a girl for her lover's indifference.

19–23. The sense is: [*Pues*] *tus ojos te eclipsan tu placer cuando, aurora de ti misma, empiezas a amanecer a tu placer,* [*que*] *se serenen tus ojos....* Her eyes eclipse her pleasure by dimming their brightness with tears. She is like the dawn because her tears are like the dew that falls at dawn.

24. *perlas:* tears.

## 12

11. *archas:* a Gallicism, alluding to the royal bodyguard of archers.

16. Because they never lack scent (*buen aire*).

25–8. *Quién...quién:* 'some...some'. Some are reluctant to reveal their love (*fe*) in case they invite the attention of the bee.

31. The bee's sting is like the sum of Cupid's darts.

35. *por señas:* 'and indeed...'.

41. *ay:* Hyacinth was transformed into a flower bearing the letters AI, Apollo's cry of grief.

45–8. The jasmine's white garb is belied by its heady scent that invites to love.

55. An allusion to the light brown bracts from which the lily's flower emerges (see Dámaso Alonso, *Góngora y el 'Polifemo'*, I, 308). The *borceguí* was a fine leather knee-boot—so the lily must be Portuguese since the Portuguese did not affect elegant or courtly footwear.

58. *quiés* = *quieres.*

65. *meninas:* young ladies-in-waiting.

72. *a dos y a tres:* in two and three parts.

73. *guardadamas:* an official 'cuyo ministerio es ir a caballo al estribo del coche de las damas quando salen fuera, para que nadie pueda llegar a hablarles' (*Diccionario de autoridades*).

75–6. The reference to *guardadamas* is doubly appropriate: the allusion is to the astringent properties of the bark and cones of the cypress, part of the stock-in-trade of the seventeenth-century Celestina for the treatment of certain female ailments.

79. *lo frío:* their unfunny humour.

84. *con:* 'although' here. *hombre de placer:* 'jester', 'buffoon'. The *estanques*, unlike jesters, are not noisy.

85–8. A complicated joke. 'In their constant demands—and not for water, for their interest is not in water (but in money); nor do they ask for what they don't drink (since they prefer wine).' *pedir:* the *estanques* invite the onlooker to take his pleasure in them; but they do not ask for water since they already have plenty.

## 13

An *a lo divino* version of an earlier pastoral *romance* by Góngora.

4. Because echoes spread the sound further abroad.

7–8. An allusion to the book sealed with seven seals in *Revelation*, v, which only the Lamb was worthy to open.

10. *que su cuna* = *cuya cuna.*

11. *Luna:* a symbol of the Virgin Mary.

12. *dos luceros:* the infant's eyes.

13–16. The sense is: *frágil choza no abrigó pastor*, [*ni*] *albergue ciego* [*abrigó*] *fiera que no penetre el cuidado...:* 'there is no shepherd in however humble a cottage, no beast in its hidden lair, but is pierced with love of the infant and a desire to see him'.

17–18. A Greek accusative. The sense is: *la diligencia, calzada—en vez de abarcas—del viento.*

20. *paraninfos:* here 'messengers of joy'.

29. *tanto...celestial:* the sense is: *tantas cosas celestiales* (or *tantos seres celestiales*).

31–2. I.e. *que hallarás claro este portal a pesar de la noche.*

## 14

4. 'Did not exempt you from being a woman' (and hence inconstant).

5. An allusion to the ermine's fabled horror of dirtying its white coat.

13–16. The oak is sturdy, but with its leaves will flirt with any breeze.

21–4. The widowed turtle-dove was a traditional symbol of constancy to its lost mate; Góngora's has remarried.

38. *interés:* 'self-interest', 'greed'. Góngora urges the shepherdess to follow her fancy at the expense of wealth.

46. *mirares al sol:* the eagle was supposed to have the ability to look at the sun without being blinded. Góngora is attempting to dissuade his *zagala* from too much constancy to one object.

50. *lasciva candidez:* because they are both white (being doves) and amorous (since they serve Venus). It is their whiteness (symbol of innocence) which the shepherdess is not to imitate.

53–6. An allusion to Echo, who succumbed to an unrequited love for Narcissus.

57–60. Góngora will proclaim her ingratitude if she persists in it.

## V 'LETRILLAS'

### 1

21–2. *El rey que rabió* figures in a number of proverbial sayings. By *las dulces patrañas del Rey que rabió* Góngora means 'time-honoured stories'.

31–3. See Introduction, p. 21.

36. Wine.

### 2

3–4. Fortune's gifts are topsy-turvy: when she should give one thing she gives another.

9. *encomiendas:* grants of land and certain privileges to members of the military orders.

10. *sambenito:* a penitential garment worn by those convicted by the Inquisition.

32. On the gibbet.

### 3

1–7. 'Not only the singing of the nightingales can be heard among the flowers: some of the music is the sound of the running stream (*campanitas de plata*), like silvery bells that greet the morning; and the humming of bees (*trompeticas de oro*), that sound like golden trumpets saluting the brightness of my beloved's eyes.' In this interpretation I follow R. Jammes, *ed. cit.*

10–11. The Sirens sang by the seashore; these Sirens, the birds, sing in a poplar grove, which Góngora describes therefore as their *húmidas espumas.*

12–13. 'If you ignore for a moment the sweet clamour of the birds' (you can hear the fainter music of the stream and the bees).

23–4. *violín que vuela...inquieta lira:* the singing birds (*inquieta:* 'restless').

34. The stream.

35–6. The bees, who hover above the jasmine, for this reason described as *coronados.*

37. *los dos hermosos corrientes:* the stream and the bees, both 'streams' of music. *Corriente* was often masculine in the seventeenth century.

38. *recuerdan gentes:* arouse people—that is, to the uninsistent music of the stream and the bees.

## 4

7–9. *cisnes...Venus:* the beauty of Menga rivals that of Venus, so that her geese can fittingly be compared with Venus' swans.

13–16. The feathers of the least handsome of the geese are so white that even he would be worthy to draw the chariot of Venus (normally drawn by doves)—Venus, born of the sea (*la que fue espuma*).

17–18. 'A shining treasure—in beauty, not in value.'

25–8. Because of the whiteness of her feet, geese and stream seem to acquire the whiteness of ivory. Note the change in the *estribillo.*

31–2. 'The whiteness of her feet seems to dissolve and form the bright waters of the stream—but it doesn't in fact.'

35–6. The *estribillo* changes once again. The sense is: 'clothing the geese with their snowy-whiteness, and lending its brightness to the stream' (as if the colour of both had its source in the whiteness of Menga's feet).

## 5

1. *clavel:* the infant Jesus.

2. *Aurora:* the Virgin Mary.

3. *heno:* the hay in the manger in which the child was laid.

5. *tenía:* 'held'.

18. Because she remained a virgin.

19. *púrpura:* the colour of kingship, appropriate to Christ the King, to whom only the most humble (symbolised by the hay) were faithful.

25. *dino* = *digno.*

29–30. The hay was at once the humble substitute for bed linen and (because of its colour) like cloth of gold for the infant King's canopy.

## 6

R. Jammes suggests (*ed. cit.* pp. 21–3) that this *letrilla* may have been composed on the occasion of an illness of the Marqués de Flores. Flores was a friend of Góngora's, and is frequently referred to in the letters. The *Flores* of the estribillo would then be a pun. If this view, to my mind a convincing one, were accepted, the poem would then be addressed ostensibly by the marigold to the other flowers of the garden but in reality to Flores, newly warned of the fragility of life.

2. *lo que va:* 'the difference between'.

3. *maravilla:* a pun: 'marigold' and 'marvel'.

19. *efímeras:* 'mayflies'—as shortlived as the flowers.

29–30. 'If amber flowers, then jasmine is its blossom.'

39–40. Because it prefers short-lived beauty to longer-lived mediocrity.

49–50. The sun grants the sunflower a longer life because the flower flatters it by always turning its face to the sun (*hojas* = 'petals' here).

## VI 'DÉCIMAS'

7–8. The sense is: *condujo* [*a una*] *fatigada cazadora, su frente* [*cubierta*] *de perlas*....

9–10. Her white skin adorned like lilies the border of the spring.

26. *sin verlas* = *sin ser vistas* (because the wings of Love and Zephyr are invisible).

39–40. The sound of the stream lulls her to sleep.

41–4. 'Just when Cupid, leaning like Narcissus over the sleeping crystal (the white form of Clori)—not over the running crystal of the spring....'

# INDEX OF TITLES AND FIRST LINES